One Love

One Love

A Pastoral Guide to
The Order of Celebrating Matrimony

Paul Turner

LITURGICAL PRESS

Collegeville, Minnesota

www.litpress.org

1	2	3	4	5	6	7	8	9

Library of Congress Control Number: 2016936472

ISBN: 978-0-8146-4923-7   978-0-8146-4948-0 (ebook)

RANDOLFO WILLIS ET MARIÆ TVRNER

CVIVS ANNI XXV MATRIMONII

SACRIFICII EXEMPLVM QVOTIDIANVM

FRVCTVVMQVE AMORIS SVPVERFLVENTIVM
PRODVXERVNT

GRATIAS AGIT AVCTOR

FRATER

Contents

Acknowledgments

I wish to thank

Doug Ferraro & Dave Holloway, who read,

Barry Hudock, who steered,

Frank Agnoli, who shared,

The people of St. Anthony Catholic Church, who sacrificed,

Bill and Alice Turner, who modeled,

God, who is one.

What Is *The Order of Celebrating Matrimony?*

T he official book used for Catholic wedding ceremonies is called *The Order of Celebrating Matrimony* (OCM). It carries the same value as other liturgical books such as the Roman Missal, the Lectionary, the *Rite of Baptism for Children*, and the *Order of Christian Funerals*. All these books and others like them contain the official prayers and rubrics for Catholic services. The Vatican still issues them all first in Latin, and then authorizes their translation into different vernacular languages around the world.

After the liturgical renewal of the Second Vatican Council, among the first ritual books to appear in English was the one for weddings. The Vatican responded favorably to a pressing pastoral need for an updated celebration of matrimony in the language of the people. That book, *Rite of Marriage*, came into use in 1969. The Vatican authorized a second Latin edition in 1990, which introduced some enhancements to the Introduction and the ceremonies. However, the English translation of this second edition was delayed for two main reasons. First, in 2001 the Vatican issued new rules for translation from Latin into all the vernacular languages. The International Commission on English in the Liturgy (ICEL), which prepares liturgical translations, had already begun work on the marriage rite under the former rules, so all its efforts had to be revised with new eyes. Second, in 2002 the Vatican published the third edition of the Roman Missal. ICEL gave its translation precedence because the Missal is arguably the most used of all Catholic liturgical books. Besides, the Missal interlocks with the marriage ceremony, so it had to be completed first before the translation of the revised book for weddings could complement it.

This second edition of the original *Rite of Marriage* became available in English throughout the United States in 2016. The Latin title had never changed, but its translation is now more literal: *The Order of Celebrating Matrimony*.

The word "order" designates an entire ceremony, of which certain parts of it may be called "rites." For example, the first part of every Mass is called "the introductory rites," but these rites form part of a complete ceremony called "the Order of Mass." The title of the wedding book now more accurately designates it as an order, like *The Order of Confirmation*. The first wedding book was called "Rite"—without the definite article. The second edition is called "The Order"—with the definite article—to clarify its official status and unique purpose.

The name for the event is now called "matrimony." The two words "marriage" and "matrimony" can be found in other official books, such as the *Catechism of the Catholic Church* and the *Code of Canon Law*. Both English words translate the same Latin word, *matrimonium*. However, "matrimony" refers to something broader than the ceremony of marriage. It expresses the entire way of life that the engaged couple desire to enter. Since the Catholic Church expects a man and a woman to make a permanent, faithful commitment to each other, open to the gift of children, church leaders sometimes find themselves promoting a specific kind of relationship to which other couples in society do not ascribe. The United States Conference of Catholic Bishops hoped that putting the word "matrimony" in the title of this book would set its Catholic meaning in relief against other usages of "marriage" in the culture.

The word "celebrating" did not appear in the first translation of the title. Few people missed it, though it had always been there in Latin. The titles of other liturgical books do not use this word. For example, *The Order of Confirmation* is the correct title, not *The Order of Celebrating Confirmation*. Its inclusion in this title demonstrates a realization that the word "matrimony" both in English and in Latin refers to more than the liturgical event. The title of this book, then, has always carried an extra word to help people understand that it describes what happens in church on the wedding day. The community celebrates a liturgy that launches matrimonial life.

"Celebrating" has another connotation, of course, namely, the special joy that fills a wedding day. From childhood, many people dream about the ceremony that will unite them to a partner for life. Once engaged, couples usually plan the event long in advance. The expense and detailed planning leading up to a wedding lack a parallel in other aspects of individual and family life. In general, people hope that the day will bring a true celebration. The Catholic Church plays a key role, housing the ceremony that ushers this day from hopes to happiness.

The English title of the book changed quite a bit, then, from *Rite of Marriage* to *The Order of Celebrating Matrimony*. The only word that remained the same in the revised edition is "of." Perhaps that is fitting. In English, "of" signifies the genitive case, the case of the apostrophe, the case of belonging. A wedding concerns two people making public their decision to belong exclusively to each other. In their longing and belonging, they are one love.

The Introduction to the OCM

M any readers skip over the introductory material of books. They care less about forewords, dedications, acknowledgments and publication data than about the content of the book they have just picked up. Consequently, some people may overlook the difference between the Introductions of the two editions of the OCM. The one in the first edition had eighteen paragraphs. The second version of the Introduction spreads over forty-four. This enhancement is one of the most substantial changes in the second edition of the OCM.

The Vatican's Congregation for Divine Worship and the Discipline of the Sacraments expanded the Introduction for several reasons. Because this book came out so early after the Second Vatican Council, its Introduction represents the first attempt at writing such an essay for a revised liturgical book. After this one, the Introductions of other rituals began to conform to a recognizable structure in four parts: "The Importance and Dignity of the Sacrament," which explains the theological framework out of which the liturgical order developed; "Duties and Ministries," which describes the various liturgical and pastoral responsibilities of the diverse ministers—and of the people of God; "The Celebration," which treated the ceremonial circumstances out of which follow the detailed rubrics to come; and "Adaptations," which surveys the adjustments to the liturgy that may be requested by conferences of bishops around the world, in order to apply them to their own cultural milieu. Such adaptations require approval from the Holy See. The original Introduction for the *Rite of Marriage* treated these themes, but not in this orderly fashion, and not in such detail. Therefore, its paragraphs have been rearranged to fit the outline of Introductions in other liturgical books.

This rearrangement uncovered areas of omission when compared to the other books. Furthermore, two new sources treating marriage and family life emerged: Within fifteen years of the publication of the *Rite of Marriage*, Pope St. John Paul II delivered his 1981 Apostolic Exhortation on the Role of the Christian Family in the Modern World, *Familiaris Consortio*. Shortly thereafter, the Vatican published its revised *Code of Canon Law* in 1983. Excerpts from these works helped fill the gaps in the Introduction to the OCM. Its original references to Vatican II's *Gaudium et Spes*, the Pastoral Constitution on the Church in the Modern World, are all still in place.

As a result, the first section of the revised Introduction, especially the first eleven paragraphs, offers a beautiful summary of the Catholic Church's teaching about marriage. It treats such themes as these:

- the covenant of matrimony "derives its force . . . from creation" and has been raised to the dignity of a sacrament;
- the couple's irrevocable consent is given freely, is lived in fidelity, and is open to the "supreme gift" of children;
- matrimony is a communion of life and love that survived original sin;
- it is a sacrament of Christ's covenant with the church;
- the joy of the wedding at Cana foreshadowed the new covenant;
- a valid marriage between a baptized man and woman is always a sacrament;
- Christian spouses participate in the "unity and fruitful love" of Christ and the church;
- the Holy Spirit helps Christian spouses;
- family life cooperates with the Creator's love;
- after the wedding, God continues to call the couple to live in marriage.

These first eleven paragraphs will reward a person who gives them a careful reading. They could form an important part of the couple's marriage preparation. With suitable explanations, these paragraphs will inspire engaged couples to the noble way of life that lies before them, a life they willfully embrace out of love, and which Christ enriches with a sacrament.

3

The Order of Blessing
an Engaged Couple

N ew to the second edition of the OCM is The Order of Blessing an Engaged Couple, located in its second appendix (218–36). Ever since 1989 a blessing of an engaged couple has been included in the Catholic Church's *Book of Blessings*, another of the official books in its liturgical library. The blessing appears there in both longer and shorter versions, but the OCM now contains a more accessible presentation of the ceremony.

It is not obligatory. No couple is required to formalize their engagement in the presence of a minister representing the church with prayers drawn from the OCM. However, they may do so. They may elect to celebrate it on their own. Or it could be appropriate as part of a parish's marriage preparation program.

This blessing is not binding. Once the couple receive it, they are not therefore canonically or legally obliged to be married. Only a marriage ceremony can be binding. The dissolution of an engagement inflicts emotional pain especially on the couple, but also on their family and friends. Even so, the breakup of an engagement is usually a better choice than the breakup of a marriage would be. The couple enter the engagement ceremony with the best of hopes and expectations. Perhaps these will not be realized. The blessing does not force them into marriage, but it does prepare a path for a bright future.

To celebrate this blessing the couple could gather relatives and friends in a family home or at some other location. The introduction prefers that one of the parents preside (219). However, a priest or deacon may lead the ceremony, or a lay minister from the parish may do so. If a priest takes the lead, he is not to combine it with Mass (221). And if a priest or a deacon presides, all present must clearly understand that this is not the wedding. A presiding lay leader helps make the distinction between this blessing and the sacrament of matrimony. When a parent presides, the ceremony more naturally shows that the engagement is affecting family systems. It also shows that married couples in those families have both opportunity and responsibility to serve as models and intercessors for the engaged.

If a layman or laywoman is to preside, an experienced presider from the parish would advisably offer training. The person should understand how to read a liturgical book, to distinguish rubrics from spoken words, to create a sense of the sacred, and to make appropriate adaptations due to the location of the celebration and the participants.

The Order of Blessing an Engaged Couple begins with the sign of the cross, and the presiding minister gives a formal greeting to the gathered assembly (222–23). The presider then delivers an introduction that explains the purpose of the gathering. The OCM scripts out a suggestion for this address, but the presider may use other similar words of introduction.

Someone proclaims a reading from Sacred Scripture. The OCM offers a selection of four possible passages (225–27). Two of these are favorites: Jesus' command to love one another, found in John's gospel, and Paul's poetic description of love from his First Letter to the Corinthians. The passage from the prophet Hosea does not share the same renown, but it supplies a moving image of God betrothing his people. Similarly, the excerpt from Paul's Letter to the Philippians receives scant notice in popular culture, but its vision of selfless community life holds the power to inspire families, parishes, and indeed any assembly of Christians. Even if a layperson presides, the gospel may be chosen, and a layperson may proclaim it.

Verses from Psalm 145 may follow the reading (228). Like the psalm in the Liturgy of the Word at Mass, this would unfold in responsorial fashion. The person leading the psalm could be a reader, a cantor, or the leader of the service. *The General Instruction of the Roman Missal* (GIRM) calls a lay minister performing this specific function "the psalmist" (61 and 99), designating the unique role of leading the people not just in any hymn or refrain, but in the proclamation of a passage from the Bible. The psalmist proclaims or sings a refrain, which all repeat, and then the psalmist chants or reads a series of verses, and all repeat the initial refrain after each group of them. Churchgoers are more accustomed to singing a psalm after the first reading and before the gospel, so having a psalm come last may seem unusual. However, the *Book of Blessings* includes many services that observe this sequence: first comes a reading, possibly drawn from the gospels. Then, to engage the voice of the gathered people, as a kind of biblical commentary upon the reading and an application of it to the specific gathering at hand, a responsorial psalm follows. In the Order of Blessing an Engaged Couple, the psalm is not obligatory. It may be replaced by another suitable song, or simply omitted.

Whenever Catholics gather for liturgical prayer, the proclamation of the word of God holds an honored place. All should listen attentively and participate when invited.

The presiding minister may share a few thoughts about the reading, in order to explain it and to apply it to the particular circumstance of engagement (229). The rubrics do not use the word "homily" because the liturgical books in general reserve that word to the reflection offered by an ordained priest or deacon. This address, which may be delivered by a lay presider, possesses a similar function. The minister preparing these thoughts would do well to keep in mind that none of the readings suggested in this Order of Blessing was originally written explicitly for engaged couples, not even the much-appropriated hymn to love from 1 Corinthians 13. The authors of the New Testament passages that appear in this section of the OCM all wrote their words for the entire Christian community to read. All Christians should have this kind of love, not just the engaged. Nevertheless, love among Christians begins with the love of families. In the context of an engagement ceremony, these readings do not so much retain their original purpose (addressing a community that fails to love fully, and urging them to love better) as much as they will serve a modern purpose (addressing a couple who succeed to love each other fully, and urging them to love more broadly). Their love should demonstrate and inspire Christian love.

After the readings and the address that follows, prayers are offered for various needs (230). These come in a structure resembling the universal prayer (also called the prayer of the faithful) at Mass. There, the priest gives the introduction, and an assisting minister lists the petitions. Something similar could be done here. The presider may deliver the introduction and then entrust the intentions to someone else. All the people respond after each petition. The presider or someone else could prepare additional petitions, or adapt the ones from the OCM to make them more personal for the engaged couple being blessed.

Then the couple may give some sign of their promise (231). They may exchange rings or some other gifts. They may sign a document. In the United States, the man probably gave a ring to the woman at the moment of their engagement, and she wears the ring from that time on. The OCM envisions that each partner may be giving a ring to the other. The presider of this ceremony may bless those rings. If the woman is already wearing her engagement ring, she may remove it, though she need not. If she does, the man may then place the ring on her finger. If she is offering him a ring, she places it on his finger.

The couple may exchange other gifts. The OCM offers no further suggestion concerning them. Whatever they are, they should fit the spirit of the ceremony, expressing its values of love, faith, and commitment.

If the couple sign a document, it cannot be a prenuptial agreement that envisions the possibility of a divorce. Some couples sign an agreement that establishes the allocation of assets in the event that the marriage fails. Such a document would question the seriousness of the commitment the couple are making. In the Catholic Church it would likely render the marriage invalid. The couple are not here to protect their own interests, but to prepare to express the full consent of their will in the wedding.

Furthermore, any signed document should not be mistaken for the wedding. This ceremony is blessing the engagement. It does not seal the marriage.

The minister blesses the gifts (232). Whether or not the couple have kept the rings on their fingers, or exchanged other gifts, or signed some kind of document, the minister's words safeguard these gifts, signifying that the couple have offered a pledge to be fulfilled in due time.

Finally, the minister blesses the couple. Two forms are given, one for a lay presider to use (233), and the other for a priest or deacon (234). Only an ordained minister blesses with a gesture, moving his hand in the form of a cross, pointed in the direction of the couple. Lay ministers are to bless without using their hand. In some cultures it is common to see parents make such a gesture over their children; however, the liturgical books consistently reserve the gesture of blessing to the hand of a deacon or priest.

The minister draws the ceremony to a conclusion (235), offering a kind of prayer over the people. All may then sing a suitable hymn (236).

The OCM does not suggest postures anywhere in this ceremony. Those familiar with postures at a Catholic Mass may wish to stand throughout, but sit in the event of a non-gospel reading and for the minister's reflection on the Scriptures. However, this ceremony may be formal or informal, and it seems to tolerate having people stand or sit throughout, depending on the circumstances of the place and persons.

As an introductory paragraph notes, this ceremony "must" be adapted to circumstances (218). The Catholic Church offers considerable flexibility on the components of this celebration, over its minister, its location, and even the decision to include it as part of a couple's path toward marriage. But the ceremony is here for those who find it attractive. Celebrated well, it can encourage parents to adopt an attitude of prayerful support, while it starts the couple's liturgical preparation for the main celebration to come.

4

The Location of the Wedding

As in the first edition, the OCM presumes that the marriage will take place in the parish of the bride or the groom (27), though the couple may obtain permission by means of the bishop and the pastor to hold the celebration in another location.

The desire to involve the parish church of the bride or groom has become increasingly idealistic, but it honors what Catholic parishes can offer at their best. Parish churches can be the religious homes where people grow in their spiritual lives from one generation to the next in the neighborhood where they live. They are places where Catholics experience their sacraments, such as baptism, first confession, First Communion, and matrimony. When active Catholic parishioners fall sick, they may rely on the help of their parish priest to anoint them. When they plan their funerals, they trust that their parish will support and care for their grieving families. Ideally, then, the location for the wedding grows out of a Catholic's long-term experience of local parish life. The parish church is the natural location where faith has grown, and where parents pass it on to their children.

In reality, though, this often does not happen. Families may not anchor themselves to one parish; they may physically move from one apartment or home to another, or, staying in the same place, they may change their allegiance over time from one parish to another. For many Catholics, parish membership is not sticky. Consequently, when the time comes to select a location for the wedding, other more dominant factors surface: the beauty of the sanctuary, the length of the church's aisle, and access to a hall for the reception. All these figure into a couple's choice for location. Rural churches sometimes see more stable membership because of the intersection of their members' civic, educational, social, and ecclesial life. But society is increasingly mobile, and people are used to shopping around to find the services they most want. They also shop for a church.

Some prefer to have the ceremony in the church of the non-Catholic partner. Sometimes that person or family is more active in their church than the Catholic family is in theirs. Or the logistical and aesthetic factors tip the preference in the direction of a non-Catholic church. In such cases, the couple desiring not to have the wedding in the parish church of one or the other need permission from the diocesan bishop. This permission must be obtained through the Catholic pastor before the wedding.

Other couples prefer not to have the ceremony inside a church at all. However, canon 1118 permits marriage in another suitable place only when the Catholic is marrying an unbaptized person. Even then the local diocese may have policies that restrict this to suitable religious space, and not, for example, outdoors.

In short, the second edition of the OCM has issued no change on directions concerning the location of the wedding, even though society has become more mobile since the first edition. Nonetheless, many parishes hope that they have played a sufficient role in the lives of the bride and groom that the couple will want the ceremony at their home church and continue to seek spiritual support from it in the years to come.

5

The Procession

The entrance procession traditionally signals the solemn beginning of the celebration of matrimony. It introduces dramatic elements—music, fashion, motion, anticipation, authority, and destiny—that bring the long anticipated wedding day into reality.

In practice, the wedding procession often takes place in this way: While the people remain seated, the priest walks from his sacristy into the sanctuary. The groom and the groomsmen enter from the same or another sacristy and take positions standing in front of the first pew on the right of the nave. An organist begins to play solo processional music. The bridesmaids walk up the aisle. Groomsmen meet them and escort them to their places for the ceremony. A flower girl and ring bearer walk up the aisle. A white runner is pulled into place. The instrumental music changes to announce the bride's entrance. She steps onto the runner, arm in arm with her father. The gathered faithful stand. Upon reaching the sanctuary the father of the bride kisses her and hands her to the groom, who escorts her to their places. Then the priest begins the ceremony.

Precious little of this can be found in the rubrics of the OCM, nor in any of the Catholic ritual books preceding it before or after the council. Any variation faces the gale force of tradition, so couples who desire to do it differently need a strong will.

The traditional procession is braced by two customs symbolizing realities that society has long abandoned. One is that on the day of the wedding the groom should not see the bride before the procession. Yet many couples cohabit before marriage, and many more will talk to each other on the day of the wedding in the hours before it begins. Still, the bride enters separately from the groom, after he has taken up his position from afar.

Second, the custom of having the father escort the bride presumes that he has a voice in choosing the groom. Some potential grooms continue the custom of asking the bride's father for her hand in marriage, but it is more common for couples to reach this decision on their own. The groom may visit the bride's father as a courtesy, perhaps asking his blessing. But rarely can a father change the plans that the couple already have underway. The wedding will blend families, but the entrance procession still expresses a belief that it is the bride's father—not the couple—who consents to the wedding.

The OCM envisions two different ways that a wedding might begin. In the first form (45–47), the entire wedding party has gathered at the door of the church—the bride and the groom together with their witnesses and the parents or principal members of the family. The priest goes there with the servers to greet this waiting community warmly. This innovative beginning actually appeared in the first edition of the OCM, though the option was not presented as explicitly as it is now. The purpose of this initial greeting is for the priest to express the church's joy and to extend a message of welcome. He thus helps the couple and the entire wedding party transition from the outside world of the busy wedding preparations and the festive gatherings of friends into a celebration of spiritual significance. In some parishes before Sunday Mass begins, the ministers who will form the procession gather for a moment of silent prayer to focus their attention on the spiritual task that lies ahead. This greeting at the door has a similar purpose. The priest invites everyone in the wedding party to set aside their worldly cares and put themselves in God's presence, in order to prepare themselves—heart, mind, and soul—for the wedding now getting underway.

After that initial greeting, a single procession starts up the aisle. The ministers and the priest lead the way, and the bride and groom come at the end.

The procession may begin as it does at any Sunday Mass. If incense is used—and it may be—a server carrying the censer enters first. Following the incense, or in the absence of it, a server carrying the cross leads the others. Two more servers may carry candles. The reader or the deacon may enter with the Book of the Gospels. Then the priest walks down the aisle. If there is a deacon, he may walk in front of or beside the priest. A parish may not have multiple servers available for weddings. But if it does, servers can add not only solemnity but also normalcy to the celebration.

Members of the wedding party and the parents may enter the procession between the priest and the couple, though this is not obligatory. Strangely, the English translation of the description of the procession (46) omits these details that are quite explicit in the Latin original of the OCM's second edition. The full description speaks of the "parents" of the couple; it makes no mention of the idea that only the father of the bride joins the procession. If this first form of the wedding procession is chosen, then the procession goes to the altar "in the customary manner." As it has been translated, it seems to imply the traditional procession, but that is impossible because the wedding party is all at the door with the priest. Instead, the liturgically "customary manner" takes place: the ministers go first, that is, the servers, the reader, the deacon, and the priest as they would for a Sunday Mass. The wedding party and family follow the priest up the aisle. The bride enters with the groom, not with her father, who has already entered with the other parents. After all, the father of the bride is not giving his consent to this wedding. The bride and groom are. They enter last.

The second form does not describe a procession at all (48–50). Instead, the priest goes to the place prepared for the couple or to his chair. The couple take their places, but the OCM does not say how they get there. This vacuum allows a range of possibilities. The wedding may get underway informally, as sometimes happens in the case of small ceremonies where only a few people witness the marriage. (Catholic convalidations of civil ceremonies sometimes occur this way, for example.) Or, since the entrance of the couple is not described, the traditional procession could be done. The priest only needs to greet the couple in the sanctuary. If he enters from the sacristy with the groom and the groomsmen and waits for the bridesmaids and the bride, the second form does not seem to mind. It just describes what happens after they all arrive in the sanctuary.

The priest is still to greet the couple warmly and share an expression of joy, but he does so at the places reserved for the couple, not at the door. If there was a procession, his warm, personal greeting follows it, whereas in the first form it preceded.

The places reserved for the couple are often set in the sanctuary, but this is not universally observed. In some cultures the bride and groom take up their positions outside the sanctuary, near, for example, where Communion is commonly distributed at the head of the center aisle. The rubrics neither promote nor forbid establishing places for the couple in the sanctuary. In the first option, they entered last in the procession, so the ministers are already in the sanctuary ahead of them. If they join them there, their presence can express the central role they will play in the celebration of this sacrament.

Nor do the rubrics mention furniture. Customarily, the bride and groom share one wide kneeler or occupy two smaller ones, but as members of the assembly, they will be invited to sit for the readings and the homily. Setting chairs at their place would be a courtesy.

Similarly, no rubrics govern the placement of the witnesses and other members of the wedding party. Some parishes customarily seat them in the first pews. Others have a sanctuary spacious enough to offer them chairs next to the bride and groom. The rubrics are silent on this. When judging the best placement of the wedding party, the central role of the bride and groom should be acknowledged. If the placement of too many witnesses in the sanctuary distracts from the celebration of the wedding—and of the Eucharist—then it would be appropriate to give the other members of the wedding party honorable seats a bit removed from the bride and groom, perhaps in the first pew.

These two forms of the introductory rites merit some discussion with the engaged couple. Some may like the idea of gathering as a group in the moments before the wedding begins so that the priest may greet them at the door of the church in anticipation of the procession. Others may prefer something more traditional, or even more informal. The OCM accommodates these wishes.

The OCM is silent about the seating of other members of the family before the procession begins. Sometimes the proper seats for grandparents, godparents, stepparents, and divorced parents, as well as the sequence of the entrance of these parties and the choice of their escort, become topics of grave concern and heated discussion. The OCM offers no guidance. It is concerned more with what happens after the congregation is seated. To avoid sparks in the supercharged atmosphere of the wedding day, couples should have these matters settled long before the ceremony begins.

6

Wedding Music

M usic for the wedding "should be appropriate and should express the faith of the Church" (30). Music at a Catholic wedding has the power to gather the voices and faith of the unique and disparate congregation summoned for this occasion. It can stir the participation of the people and focus their attention on matters divine. The robust singing of a congregation can bolster the confidence of the couple. It can evangelize those who are unchurched. It can render God fitting praise.

However, like the Catholic wedding procession, Catholic wedding music contends with strong societal traditions. People usually expect to hear solos at weddings. Instrumental music normally accompanies the processions in and out of the church. A soloist may sing a traditional selection such as Schubert's *Ave Maria*, or modern popular selections that relate to the couple's romance. The OCM envisions a different approach.

The simplest way to envision the selection of music for a Catholic wedding is to review what a congregation sings on a typical Sunday—hymns, psalms, responsories, acclamations, and dialogues.

Both forms of the introductory rites envision that the entrance chant takes place after the priest privately greets and welcomes the bride and groom (46 and 50). "Entrance Chant" is the expression the Missal uses for what is commonly called the "opening hymn." The OCM borrows the same terminology. The Missal uses "Entrance Chant" to refer to several different possibilities. The GIRM explains that "chant" and "hymn" are only two of them (48).

First, the entrance chant may be a musical setting—or even a recitation—of an antiphon from the Missal. It need not be a "chant" in the style of a Gregorian chant. It could be any musical setting in any style of the words that appear in the Missal. For weddings, an antiphon opens each of the three sets of Mass texts titled "For the Celebration of Marriage," the fifth set within its collection of ritual Masses found near the back of the Missal. These antiphons are rarely used, but they supply a valuable source for thinking about the sacred words proper to a wedding Mass. If the community, choir, or cantor does not have access to or know how to sing a musical setting of these words from the Missal, or if, in the judgment of those preparing the wedding, sung music would be difficult to execute at this point for any reason, any one of these three antiphons could be recited by the priest, a reader, the congregation, or a small group within the congregation.

Second, the entrance chant may be some other psalm or antiphon. Prior to the Second Vatican Council, specific antiphons were assigned to the days and occasions of life in the church. There were no options. But the council authorized unprecedented variety in the choice of antiphons for the entrance—and the communion—of the Mass. Therefore, if people knew a musical setting of a different antiphon or even a psalm appropriate to the celebration, it is perfectly acceptable for them to sing that.

Or the entrance chant may be some other hymn. This option is the most typical for a Sunday assembly. People sing a song that helps them connect to the day, season, or occasion on which they have gathered.

There are many options. In truth, many people—musicians included—do not pay much attention to the entrance chant that appears in the Missal, but it may be a gem overlooked in liturgical planning.

There are difficulties with inviting people to sing a hymn or an antiphon, of course. In some parishes, the singing on any day is not very strong, and planning wedding music to model the Sunday assembly's song lends little appeal. Furthermore, the particular group of people gathering for the wedding have probably never before been at the same place at the same time in their lives, much less at a Catholic wedding where they are expected to sing aloud together. Nonetheless, with a good song leader and strong accompaniment, an opening hymn can put everyone in a sacred state of mind at the start of the ceremony. Some may object that many of the people in attendance do not regularly participate at Catholic worship, yet those who participate at worship in other Christian assemblies may actually sing better than Catholics do.

If an entrance song accompanies the procession, it will be more natural for people to stand from its beginning, not just for the entrance of the bride. A song of praise to God on their lips will help them focus their heart. They are here not just to watch a wedding; they are here to witness it and to worship the living God.

The second form of the introductory rites calls for the entrance chant after the members of the wedding party have arrived at their places, and the priest has greeted the couple. If instrumental music accompanied the procession and no words were sung, some form of the entrance chant takes place after the priest greets the couple in the sanctuary. The same options explained above apply: all may sing an antiphon or a hymn, or one or more people may recite the antiphon.

The ritual Mass for celebrating marriage now calls for a Gloria. This was true before the council, but the practice fell into disuse. Now the Gloria has been reinstated. As will be seen, there are some days when the ritual Mass for celebrating marriage is replaced with another Mass, but most of those occasions will call for a Gloria anyway. If the parish has one or more settings of the Gloria in repertoire, this will provide another opportunity for all to sing a song together. In the event that the special congregation assembled for the wedding does not know a musical setting of the Gloria, a cantor could lead one that invites the people to sing a refrain. Or the people could all be invited to recite the Gloria together. This does not do justice to its nature as a hymn, but depending on the assembly, it may draw the participants together by giving them a task more easily accomplished: a communal recitation of a prayer of praise.

The OCM places particular emphasis on singing the responsorial psalm (30). This requires the presence not of a stereotypical wedding soloist to sing it all, but a psalmist who leads the people in a refrain, alternating with verses. As mentioned above, this is often the same person as the cantor or song leader, but the psalmist, who takes part in the Liturgy of the Word, may use the ambo, whereas the cantor, who may lead singing at other times during the Mass, does not. This emphasis on the psalm gives some indication of how the OCM conceives wedding music. It is not decorative. It is integral. It draws people into the celebration.

A song leader may be especially helpful at a wedding. If the people in attendance are expected to sing, a good song leader can give them confidence, as well as cues. A song leader draws the people into participation much more than a wedding soloist can.

As will be seen, the congregation may sing an acclamation after the couple exchange their consent, and all may sing a hymn after the couple exchange rings. These musical elements allow the community to underscore the sacredness of celebrating matrimony, while expressing its joy and worship.

The OCM includes musical settings of the nuptial blessing (205–9), which shows an interest in both a style of music and a specific occasion in which something may be sung. Few people think of the priest or deacon as the musical soloist at a wedding, but he may enhance the celebration through prayerful chant.

The Introduction lists music as one of the elements that may be chosen together with the engaged couple (29). They may have specific ideas about wedding music, but a good pastoral staff will be able to give them guidance. This catechesis should help the couple rethink the meaning of a Catholic wedding. It is not a mere celebration of their love, but of God's love for them.

The Presider's Introduction

New to the Catholic wedding ceremony is a suggested address the priest may say publicly near the beginning of the celebration (52–53). Two samples are given, and he is free to use one or the other, or to adapt them as he sees fit. The first is addressed to the entire assembly; the second sample is addressed only to the couple. The possibility of giving such an introduction has always been in place, but the OCM now demonstrates ways it may be done.

A similar introduction may take place at any Mass (GIRM 31). Mass should begin with the entrance hymn, the sign of the cross, and the greeting. After the people answer, "And with your spirit," the priest may say a few words about the Mass of the day. He may greet groups who are present or say something about the nature of the celebration, for example. In fact, a deacon or another minister may give this introduction. Some priests do this before the sign of the cross, but the rubrics clearly state that the comments follow the greeting. The first words he says are sacred. All is placed under the sign of the cross. And by greeting the people with a phrase such as "The Lord be with you," the priest shows respect for them and engages them in sacred conversation from the very beginning of the service. Only then does he use his own words, once all the proper introductions have been made.

In theory, another minister could address the community at a wedding because that may happen at any Mass. The deacon, a catechist, the couple who helped with marriage preparation, or members of the families could say something to the couple or to the entire assembly after the priest gives the greeting. But perhaps there is some wisdom in having the priest himself give the introduction as well, as the OCM states. The people coming to a wedding are an intentional and transitory community.

The priest's introduction can anchor their relationship with him and with one another for the duration of the ceremony. These words extend the purpose of the welcome he addressed more privately to the couple and the wedding party earlier. Now he extends the same cordiality to the entire assembly. He also explains the purpose of the gathering, so that everyone knows why they are here and what is expected of them.

If the congregation has not sung an opening hymn for a wedding Mass, one of the options that accounts for the entrance antiphons may be used by the priest to incorporate it into his introductory remarks (GIRM 48). In some way, that is what these sample introductions do. They each rely on biblical passages, especially from the book of Psalms, to welcome the assembly and to situate the purpose of their gathering. These samples demonstrate one way that an antiphon can be incorporated into the opening address when the people have not sung a hymn.

Some priests give a more expansive introduction in order to welcome those who may not be familiar with Catholic worship. They may explain such matters as posture and gesture, where to find the order of service and their responses to the dialogues, and the rules governing the reception of Communion. He could do this, but the sample introductions in the OCM focus on other matters. If broader remarks seem necessary, perhaps the song leader or another representative from the parish could make them before the service begins. Or the pertinent information could be placed in a participation aid prepared for this event. Normally, a presider will find that less is more. The fewer words he says, the weightier they all become.

The Readings and Prayers

The proper selection of readings and prayers to be used at a wedding Mass is more difficult than it may appear. On the surface, the process is complicated only by the vast array of selections in the OCM (144–87). These duplicate the selections in the *Lectionary for Mass* (801–5), except for OCM 158 (Eph 4:1-6), which can be found in the weekday Lectionary for Friday of the Twenty-Ninth Week in Ordinary Time of Year II (477). In the American edition of the OCM, all the readings are published in Chapter IV. The wedding Lectionary offers nine options from the Old Testament, seven possible responsorial psalms, fourteen selections from the New Testament epistles and the book of Revelation, four verses to consider as a gospel acclamation, and ten passages from the gospels. These readings provide an embarrassment of riches.

New to the second edition of the OCM is the asterisk that appears in front of some of these citations. They mark the readings that explicitly speak of marriage, and not just of a more generic command, such as love of neighbor. A new rubric found in the opening of Chapter IV just before OCM 144 requires that one of the readings with an asterisk be proclaimed at a wedding Mass. This will help ensure that the community hears the biblical background for the Catholic celebration of matrimony.

The wedding may include one or two readings before the gospel; that is, it may follow the structure of the Liturgy of the Word provided for weekdays or Sundays. If there are two readings before the gospel, it is better to have two readers. If the responsorial psalm is not sung, another reader may lead it. The second edition of the OCM has not changed this.

The presidential prayers also come with options. There are six for the collect, two for the blessing of rings, three for the prayer over the offerings, three possible prefaces, three different nuptial blessings, three options for the prayers after Communion, and three for the final blessing. These can be mixed and matched, even though the principal prayers are grouped in the Missal in three sets.

The OCM recommends that the couple be involved in choosing from among the options for the Scripture readings, the blessing of the rings, and the nuptial blessing (29). If the couple take some time especially with the Scriptures, they will compose themselves more spiritually for the wedding. By studying the nuptial blessings, they prepare for the day when they will hear the one they choose as a newly married couple.

At first, then, the most complicated part about choosing the readings and prayers is discerning which of the many options best suit one particular couple. However, there is a preliminary question: Is the ritual Mass for celebrating marriage allowed on the day the couple have selected for their wedding?

This concern arises only in the instance when the wedding takes place during Mass. If the wedding takes place in a ceremony outside of Mass, then the planners have complete freedom to select readings and prayers from the OCM. A wedding during Mass, though, is subject to the rules of the calendar as presented in the Table of Liturgical Days in the front of the Missal. The ritual Mass for celebrating marriage is not allowed on any of the days that fall within the first four of the thirteen categories on the table (34).

Here is the ranking of days from that part of the table:

1. The Paschal Triduum of the Passion and Resurrection of the Lord.

2. The Nativity of the Lord, the Epiphany, the Ascension, and Pentecost.
   Sundays of Advent, Lent, and Easter.
   Ash Wednesday.
   Weekdays of Holy Week from Monday up to and including Thursday.
   Days within the Octave of Easter.

3. Solemnities inscribed in the General Calendar, whether of the Lord, of the Blessed Virgin Mary, or of Saints.
   The Commemoration of All the Faithful Departed.

4. Proper Solemnities, namely:
   a) The Solemnity of the principal Patron of the place, city, or state.
   b) The Solemnity of the dedication and of the anniversary of the dedication of one's own church.
   c) The Solemnity of the Title of one's own church.

d) The Solemnity either of the Title
>   or of the Founder
>   or of the principal Patron of an Order or Congregation.

Regarding the first group, it should surprise no one that a wedding scheduled for Easter Sunday would have to use the readings of Easter. It is
not permitted to celebrate Mass or sacraments on Good Friday or Holy
Saturday, and so a wedding is prohibited on those days.

The second group includes Christmas, which again offers no surprise.
The listing mentions a number of weekdays when weddings are unlikely,
such as Ash Wednesday or the first part of Holy Week. However, this
group also includes a number of Sundays that exclude the ritual Mass
for celebrating marriage: Epiphany, Ascension (in those places where
it is celebrated on a Sunday), and Pentecost, as well as the Sundays of
Advent, Lent, and Easter and the weekdays of the octave of Easter,
which would include the Saturday after Easter. Therefore, any Saturday
night wedding Mass during a season like Advent or Easter falls under
this second group. A wedding may take place on those days during Mass,
but the priest is to use the presidential prayers of the pertinent Sunday.

The third group includes days such as the Immaculate Conception (December 8), which would affect any wedding scheduled on that date. In a
year when December 8 falls on a Saturday, for example, an early afternoon
wedding at a Mass would use the prayers and readings of the holy day.

The fourth group includes some days that pertain to the local church
building where the wedding will take place. If your church is named
St. Anthony, for example, and an early afternoon wedding is set for June
13 in a year when it falls on a Saturday, the priest is to use the presidential prayers for St. Anthony, which is a solemnity only in that parish
church. The same applies to the anniversary of the day of the dedication
of the church where the wedding is taking place. If the couple happen
to pick a day that falls on that anniversary, the priest leads the Mass for
the Common of the Dedication of a Church: On the Anniversary of the
Dedication, found in the Missal under Commons, right after the Proper
of Saints. Many of the days in these four groups call for the community
to recite the profession of faith. If so, they would do so at the wedding
Mass (69). However, because the universal prayer is part of the wedding
ceremony, it displaces the Creed. On Sundays, the Creed precedes the
prayer of the faithful, but at weddings it follows, as it does, for example,
in the scrutiny Masses of the Rite of Christian Initiation of Adults.

The same rules govern the Scripture readings for any day within the same four groups of the Table of Liturgical Days. However, because catechesis on marriage is so important, one reading from the wedding Lectionary may replace one of the assigned readings on days when the ritual Mass for celebrating marriage is not said (34). Logically, this would be one of the readings that carries an asterisk from Chapter IV of the OCM.

The dependence of wedding Masses on the liturgical calendar will seem puzzling to many engaged couples, parish musicians, wedding coordinators, as well as many deacons and priests. However, a wedding is never an isolated event in the lives of two people. It takes place within the larger mystery of the church and the world. Just as a couple getting married in the United States on July 4 knows that they must conform with other civic celebrations, so a couple marrying on one of the church's holy days will blend their celebration with the observance made by the broader Catholic community.

With regard to the readers at a wedding Mass, many couples want to invite one or more of their friends or family to proclaim the Scriptures. Those who serve in these ministries at weddings provide a rich service to the gathered community. However, at times the reader with a qualifying personal relationship is inexperienced in proclaiming readings publicly in church. In anticipation of the wedding, a reader from the parish may rehearse the selected readers inside the building, from the ambo, and with the microphone, so that they can test the strength of the mic and learn how to use it effectively. Readers should also be instructed how to find the readings in the Lectionary and to proclaim them from that book, not from a photocopy. The Introduction to the *Lectionary for Mass* stresses this point (37). Often the readers for special events such as these will obtain a copy of their reading for the purpose of practice. This is a good idea, but the actual proclamation should take place from the Lectionary, not from a single sheet of paper. The liturgical book has dignity, and it is one of the symbols that give the liturgy its power. The word of God will not look powerful when proclaimed from a folded piece of paper. Before the wedding begins, readers should locate the reading in the parish Lectionary at the ambo.

If the priest or deacon wishes to proclaim the gospel from the Book of the Gospels, he should ensure that the passage is there. Most editions only have the gospels for Sundays and solemnities. Sometimes the gospel for the wedding Mass is in that book, but the minister may have to check the index to locate it and mark it with the ribbon before the ceremony begins.

Sometimes the couple would like to choose one or more readers who are close to them, but are not Catholic. According to the Directory for the Application of Principles and Norms on Ecumenism, only Catholics proclaim the readings at a Mass. However, in exceptional circumstances and for a just cause, the bishop may permit the member of another church to perform this task (133). Perhaps a wedding is such an occasion. Local diocesan regulations should give guidance for particular circumstances.

9

The Consent

At the heart of the ceremony is the exchange of consent. Many people refer to this as the "vows," but the Catholic liturgical books never use that word for what the bride and groom say to each other when they marry. According to the *Catechism of the Catholic Church*, a vow is an act of devotion made to God (2102). It is used, for example, when nuns, religious brothers, and priests commit to a community such as the Franciscans, Benedictines, or Jesuits. Members of religious orders make vows. During a wedding, the bride and groom are doing something else. They are exchanging their willful consent to each other.

The rubrics ask all to stand for this consent. This may cause problems for visibility, but the posture indicates that all serve as witnesses to the sacred act about to take place before them.

The rubrics do not say where the minister and the couple should stand for the consent. Traditionally the minister positions himself between the couple and the altar. Alternatively, the minister could stand between the couple and the people. This turns the couple's faces toward the assembly and sets the minister closer to the other witnesses.

The consent has three parts. First, the minister asks the couple a series of questions to ensure that they understand what they are about to do (60). Then they exchange their consent (62–63). Finally, the minister officially receives the consent that the couple have made (64). Some of the words for this part of the Catholic wedding changed with the second edition of the OCM in English.

In the questions, for example, the minister used to ask the couple if they have come "freely and without reservation to give yourselves to each other in marriage." Now he asks, "have you come here to enter into Marriage / without coercion, / freely and wholeheartedly?" The revised question makes some precisions. It is dealing with a canonical regulation that a person cannot enter a valid marriage if he or she is being coerced (canon 1103). Marriage is a free act of the will. This question is one reason why the rubrics for the entrance procession at a Catholic wedding do not request that the father of the bride walk her down the aisle and hand her to the groom, and why the minister does not formally ask, "Who gives this woman to be married to this man?" The decision to marry is not the father's. It must be a free expression of the will of the bride and the groom. Also, the revised translation of this question includes the word "wholeheartedly," which is asking about the couple's fidelity to each other. Marriage is to be a permanent partnership between the husband and wife (canon 1096 §1).

The second question used to be, "Will you love and honor each other as man and wife for the rest of your lives?" Here is the revised translation: "Are you prepared, as you follow the path of Marriage, / to love and honor each other / for as long as you both shall live?" Again, the question is a little fuller, and it expresses the important concern about the permanence of the relationship. Canon 1096 §1 requires the intent of a permanent union into the future. The question is, "Are you prepared?" The minister is ascertaining if the couple have the proper disposition to enter into a permanent union. Their consent will require love and honor for the rest of their lives. The revised translation avoids the previous expression "man and wife," which some have criticized as needlessly sexist. (If she is his "wife," then he is her "husband"—not just a "man.") Neither edition of the Catholic marriage rite has included the word "obey" in this question. The Catholic minister does not ask the wife to promise to obey her husband. Rather, the ceremony builds upon the presumption that each partner is equal in responsibility to the other.

The third question concerns children, and it may be omitted if circumstances warrant, for example, if the couple are advanced in years. It may not be omitted, however, if the couple prefer not to have children. Couples capable of becoming parents and choosing not to do so cannot enter matrimony in the Catholic Church (canon 1101 §2). The first English translation had the minister ask this: "Will you accept children lovingly from God, and bring them up according to the law of Christ and his Church?" Now the translation has been revised: "Are you prepared to accept children lovingly from God / and to bring them up / according to the law of Christ and his Church?" Only the opening words differ. Like the previous question, this one asks if the couple are prepared. All of these questions are meant to ascertain the state of mind of the couple before they pronounce their mutual consent.

Strangely, the first edition of the *Rite of Marriage* after Vatican II never scripted out the answers each party makes to these questions. Now, they appear in the book. Each should answer "I am" to each of the questions about their readiness, and each should respond separately. The couple may spontaneously give their answers together, but the rubric specifies several times that they each respond separately (60). The minister waits for each response before moving to the next question.

The minister summarizes the responses with the words, "it is your intention to enter the covenant of Holy Matrimony." This is a slightly expanded version of the earlier translation, which simply referred to their "intention to enter into marriage." This will be a covenant, a word deliberately chosen to distinguish the agreement from a contract. A covenant is built on the desire for one person to do for the other, even more than the other can do for the one. This imitates to some degree the covenant that Christ established with the church. It is not a contract of equal exchange. It is a selfless expression of love.

As in the first edition, the minister asks the couple to join their right hands. This gesture dates back to the very early days of Roman history. Some ancient stone sarcophagi of married couples, for example, bear carvings that show a couple joining their right hands. In some traditions the father took the hand of his daughter and placed it into the hand of the groom. The Catholic ceremony includes no such action involving the father. Instead, the bride and the groom give their hands to each other. Again, this gesture expresses their free consent.

The words of consent, the heart of the ceremony, come next (61–62). These have been slightly amended. For example, formerly each one said, "I promise to be true to you," but now the word "true" has been replaced with the word "faithful," a more direct description of what makes this relationship true. As with the questions before the consent, the couple are expressing permanence and fidelity in these revised words: "I, N., take you, N., to be my wife (husband). / I promise to be faithful to you, / in good times and in bad, / in sickness and in health, / to love and to honor you / all the days of my life."

In the United States, another traditional formula may be used: "I, N., take you, N., for my lawful wife (husband), / to have and to hold, / from this day forward, / for better, for worse, / for richer, for poorer, / in sickness and in health, / to love and to cherish, / until death do us part." This formula appeared in the first translation, though without the phrase "to love and to cherish." Because of its historical standing in the culture, this form of consent has won the Vatican's approval again as an alternate. Its inclusion of the word "lawful" shows its legal origins.

For pastoral reasons, the couple may give their consent by responding to a question instead of reciting the entire formula. The minister reads the words of consent in question form from the OCM, first to the groom and then to the bride, and each answers, "I do." The minister may use the questions based on either of the two forms of consent (63).

Commonly, though, the minister states the words of consent phrase by phrase, first for the groom, and then for the bride. Each repeats the phrases after the minister. Although this is common, the rubrics never indicate it should or even may be done. Sometimes there are practical difficulties; for example, the congregation and the witnesses may not hear the words of consent clearly unless the couple are miked. The rubrics seem to envision that a minister holds the book up between the couple, turning it first to the groom in such a way that he can read the words while looking at the bride, and then turning the book to the bride so that she similarly can read while addressing the groom. Some couples memorize the words of consent. After all, these are the words by which they will live as a couple. They may want to know them well enough to say them out loud without support. All these solutions are acceptable. Most importantly, the couple need to speak their consent aloud, the words expressing the desire in their hearts.

Because all present are witnesses, they need to hear these words. Some couples are timid, especially on the wedding day, and in nervousness may speak their consent softly. Perhaps in marriage preparation they can be encouraged to speak in confidence and clearly so that all may hear their commitment. In some parishes, the groom wears a lapel mic that will pick up the voices of the couple. Or another minister stands nearby with a microphone judiciously placed where it picks up the couple's voices. These are the most important words in the sacrament of matrimony; making them audible will be worth the effort.

The minister then receives the consent. This appeared in the first edition as well, but now the OCM gives him two options (64). They basically express the same point: The minister asks God to strengthen the couple's consent. The first version prays for God to bring his blessing to fulfillment. The second option is the new one. It expresses more about who this God is—the God of the ancestors who joined together the first couple, Adam and Eve. This bride and groom join the list of their successors. Both versions recall Jesus' words that no one should put asunder what God has joined (Mark 10:9 and Matt 19:6).

Also new to the second edition of the OCM, a dialogue between the minister and the people immediately follows the reception of consent: The minister says, "Let us bless the Lord." All respond, "Thanks be to God." The people may use a different acclamation (65). This will work best if the people sing it, but they may recite their words. As a comparison, at one point in an ordination Mass, the bishop formally announces that he chooses the candidates for the priesthood. All answer, "Thanks be to God." In the United States the people then may applaud. Applause, whether at an ordination or perhaps at a wedding, should not be interpreted as praise for the couple as much as thanks to God. It may express the communal joy of this day. God has brought this bride and groom together. God deserves the thanks.

The OCM lists the options for the form of consent as a part of the service from which the engaged couple help make a choice (29). If they take some time reviewing these words, they will come to greater understanding of the meaning of the ceremony and the life of matrimony.

10

The Rings

For the ring ceremony, both the bride and the groom give a ring to each other (66–67A). Prior to the liturgical reforms, the groom alone gave a ring to the bride. The mutual exchange of rings is another sign of the equality expected in fulfilling the roles of husband and wife.

The second edition of the OCM has introduced slight variations to this part of the ceremony. The minister will see a fresh translation of all the options for blessing the rings (66, 194, and 195). The main change in their wording brings forward the notion of "faithfulness." The rings express the unique fidelity that each partner will observe for the sake of the other.

The minister may sprinkle the rings with blessed water. This sprinkling was part of the ceremony during the many centuries before the Second Vatican Council, but then it was removed from the revised liturgy. Nonetheless, after the council many priests and deacons continued sprinkling rings in the absence of the rubric. The second edition of the OCM now includes the sprinkling as an option.

As the groom gives a ring to the bride, he says, "N., receive this ring / as a sign of my love and fidelity. / In the name of the Father, and of the Son, / and of the Holy Spirit." The bride repeats these words as she places the other ring on the groom's finger. The only difference in this revised translation is the change from the word "take" to "receive." Each of them "receives" a ring from the other. They do not "take" it. Each receives the gift of faithfulness that the other willfully offers.

As with the exchange of consent, the groom and bride have customarily repeated their lines phrase by phrase after the priest or deacon. But there are other options. They may memorize these words. Or they may read them directly from the book, held in a way that they can see the face of their partner while they say the words and position the ring.

The priest or deacon is the church's official witness to the exchange of the couple's consent. The couple in a sense administer this sacrament to each other, but their words require the presence of the church's minister. Therefore, the minister has a key role but should not usurp the primary role of the couple. If the minister says the words of consent for the couple to repeat, and if the minister says the words concerning the exchange of the rings for the couple to repeat, the minister may be placing himself in a more central role than the liturgy envisions. The priest or deacon should be careful not to draw too much attention to himself.

The options for the blessing of rings is another part of the service from which the engaged couple may help make a choice (29). It would benefit them to study these prayers and make a selection from among them, in order to appreciate more deeply the significance of the rings.

After the exchange of the rings, all may sing a hymn of praise (68). This would again turn the attention of the community toward God, whose wondrous love has joined this couple in holy matrimony. The hymn is deferred a few moments if the celebration includes the *arras*.

11

The *Arras*, the *Lazo*, and the Veil

Among the customs popular in places such as Mexico and the Philippines are the *arras*, the *lazo*, and the veil. The revised American edition of the OCM makes these available within the ritual book in English for the first time. They have been available in the United States in Spanish since 2010.

The *arras* or coins have long been associated with the exchange of rings, so that is why they appear in conjunction with that ceremony. Originally they symbolized the new husband's pledge to provide for the needs of his wife. Like the single ring ceremony, at first it denoted a one-way gift. Now, the ceremony of the *arras* has been reinterpreted as another symbol of mutuality.

Often the engaged couple designate another couple to serve as the *padrinos* or sponsors of the *arras*. If so, the *padrinos* step forward at this time and present the boxed coins to the minister for the blessing.

The minister asks God to bless the coins (67B). The rubric makes no mention of sprinkling blessed water; that appears only for the blessing of the rings, and even there the sprinkling is optional. However, people from cultures that broadly popularize the devotional usage of blessed water may argue for its inclusion with the *arras*. Still, the ritual's omission of sprinkling here may attempt to deflect attention away from the coins and toward the rings, which remain the central physical symbols of the Catholic wedding.

The husband hands the *arras* to his wife. The box traditionally holds thirteen coins, which he pours into her hands. The number of coins apparently represents what is sometimes called a "baker's dozen," that is, a symbol of plenitude. The words of the groom are a translation of those included in the Spanish-language ceremony in the United States:

"N., receive these *arras* as a pledge of God's blessing / and a sign of the good gifts we will share." The word *arras* comes from a word meaning "pledge," and these words shift the meaning away from the husband pledging material support for the wife, and toward a celebration of God's pledge to bless them with many good gifts. The words imply spiritual gifts, not merely material ones. After the wife receives these coins, she pours them back into the hands of her husband while reciting the same words and addressing him by name.

Once again, the couple may repeat the words after the priest or deacon, memorize them, or read them from the book. As with the consent and the exchange of rings, the rubric implies that the couple read their lines while the minister's voice remains silent.

After the exchange of the *arras* the people may sing the hymn of praise that otherwise concludes the exchange of rings (68).

The *lazo* is a double cord that wraps around the new husband and wife. It may resemble a large figure eight, or even a double rosary. As with the *arras*, another couple designated as *padrinos* of the *lazo* may bring it forward for the blessing and then place it over the heads of the couple.

Alternatively, or subsequently, other *padrinos* may present a veil for a blessing, and then hold it over the newlyweds. Or, if there is no separate veil, they may grasp the hem of the bride's veil and pin it to the shoulder of the groom.

The ceremonies for blessing and placing the *lazo* and the veil may happen before the nuptial blessing (71B). The rubric is not strict because customs vary. However, the OCM envisions that the newlyweds kneel after the Lord's Prayer while the *padrinos* bring forward the *lazo* and/or the veil. These articles are blessed as "a symbol of the indissoluble union" the couple make with God's help. The minister uses the same words to bless the *lazo* and the veil, except for the name of the item. The rubrics do not include a sprinkling with blessed water. Again, this probably helps make a contrast between these momentary symbols and the rings that will endure as the permanent sign of marriage.

The OCM does not indicate when these items are removed. Logically, though, this happens after the nuptial blessing. Once the blessing is completed, the *padrinos* would remove the *lazo* and/or the veil, or they unpin the veil from the groom. The couple could then stand more freely for the sign of peace.

12

Other Wedding Customs

Other customs from outside this ritual may become traditional. For example, after Communion at some weddings, the Catholic bride carries flowers to the church's statue of the Blessed Virgin Mary and places them at the image's feet. The practice is not mentioned in the rubrics of a Catholic wedding, yet many people presume that it should be done. In some cases the groom accompanies the bride to the statue, though this action is a later development in the tradition. His presence probably shows the influence of words and symbols of equality in the ceremony. This kind of practice continues under the force of a statement in the Introduction to the OCM that "attention should also be given . . . to local customs, which may be observed if appropriate" (29).

Of course, that statement opens the door to a lot of other practices because of the difficulty in defining what is a "custom"—and even what is "local."

The unity candle, for example, enjoys wide usage. In practice, a pillar candle is set on a side table in or near the sanctuary with a smaller candle on each side. (It should not be placed on the altar, which is reserved for items pertaining to the Liturgy of the Eucharist. This will be explained later in the commentary about signing the wedding record.) Customs vary, but sometimes the parents of the couple light the side candles, representing the two families, upon entering the church. Then, following the blessing and exchange of rings, the bride and groom go to those candles, and together use them to light the central one.

Something about this ritual has spoken deeply to the many couples who request it for their ceremony. One also sees variations on it. For example, sometimes they light the paschal candle as their unity candle, though the Missal does not foresee this as one of the paschal candle's usages. The paschal candle brightens the Easter season with its message of death and resurrection, and it burns at baptisms as well as funerals. In another variation, the couple extinguish the family candles once the unity candle has been lighted, but this may send a disturbing signal that families are being eliminated rather than integrated. Symbols are tricky. Compared to the rings, which will long endure, a candle is designed to melt away. But the persistent usage of a unity candle at weddings gives evidence that it speaks something meaningful to the hearts of the engaged.

Couples may request other symbols that they have witnessed in the weddings of friends and family. Some of these symbols may be quite common, such as the traditional wedding procession, which could be viewed as one expression of the local customs covered by OCM 29. During the sign of peace some couples present flowers to their mothers. Such requests are not surprising.

Other symbols may be unknown to the minister and parish staff. Authorities in each parish may need to exercise considerable judgment to determine if the couple's request for something extra fits the embrace of a local custom. Ministers should also be careful that they do not forbid an option simply because it is not their personal preference. Sometimes couples propose legitimate ideas that may be unusual but are not contrary to the liturgy. Compassionate ministers will approach these with an open mind.

The highlights of the wedding ceremony are the exchange of consent and of the rings. Whatever else is added to the ritual should not distract the couple or the congregation from these central elements, nor diminish their importance.

13

The Universal Prayer

A wedding will include the universal prayer, also called the prayer of the faithful (69). As with the petitions of any celebration, this list of intentions invites the gathered faithful to offer their prayers to God.

This feature has been included in weddings ever since the Second Vatican Council, but the OCM now includes samples in its first appendix. As always, these may be adapted or replaced by a new composition.

The GIRM lists four categories to keep in mind: the needs of the church, public authorities and the salvation of the whole world, those burdened by any kind of difficulty, and the local community (70). The list of petitions should always express concerns in all those areas.

A couple could profitably spend some time of their marriage preparation thinking about these petitions. Who is coming to their wedding? What concerns will they bring? As the couple think about the love that they have for each other, what do they wish for the rest of their guests? for the church? for the community where they will live? for the rest of the world?

Among the manifold items requiring plans before a wedding, the universal prayer often gets scant attention. The samples provided in the appendix to the OCM will give guidance, but unless they are adapted, they may become overused. The nature of these petitions is that they specify the local community's needs and its perceptions of the needs of others. Just as the preacher tries to personalize the homily for the couple, so the parish can also personalize the petitions.

It takes work. Not everyone has the skill of writing prose. However, if people with that skill could spend time with the couple discerning their concerns and hopes for the future, they could then gather a list of intentions and craft them beautifully for the celebration. Engaged couples typically consult experts in fashion, stationery, and pastries. They could also seek the service of those who can write prayerful prose.

The universal prayer is among the parts of the wedding that the Introduction to the OCM suggests the couple help plan (29).

14

The Procession of the Gifts

A s in the previous edition, the OCM says that the bride and groom may bring the bread and wine to the altar if this seems appropriate (70).

Unquestionably it would be appropriate if both the bride and the groom are Catholics who will be receiving Communion at the wedding Mass. The eucharistic liturgy implies a link between the presentation of the gifts and the reception of Communion. At any Mass, the gifts are a symbol of the people in the assembly, who are offering their lives to God in hopes that their sacrifice will be acceptable. During the eucharistic prayer the priest prays for the bread and wine to become the Body and Blood of Christ. These gifts, then, are returned, consecrated, for the communion of the people who offered them.

There are logistical difficulties. Often before Mass the bread and wine are set on a small table near the entrance of the church, nowhere near the place established for the bride and groom during the wedding Mass. It may seem awkward for them to go down the aisle to pick up the gifts and bring them to the sanctuary. Indeed, sometimes the bride's gown includes a train, which attendants may hold to help her make graceful turns.

Alternatively, others could bring the gifts from the back of the church to the bride and groom in or near the sanctuary, who then present them to the priest. Or, for the sake of this one Mass, the bread and wine could be set beforehand near the place prepared for the couple. The gifts would lose some of their significance as offerings that come from the gathered assembly, but their location would shorten the distance for the couple to walk.

The rubric invites the couple to bring the gifts "to the altar" (70). For a typical Mass the GIRM states that members of the faithful bring the gifts to "an appropriate place" (73, 178). Often, that is interpreted to mean at the edge of the sanctuary. But it could mean the altar. It is hard to know how to read this discrepancy. Was it just an oversight in a book first published early in the liturgical renewal? Or do the circumstances of the wedding aim to draw more significance out of having the newlyweds specifically approach the altar near the beginning of the Liturgy of the Eucharist?

In any event, if the bride and groom present the bread and wine, they are symbolizing the profound offering of their own lives together with the bread and wine placed on the altar of sacrifice. They already hold a sacrificial love for each other. They are dedicating that love as an offering to God at this Mass. The priest and the people will pray that the sacrifice of the couple's lives may be acceptable to God, the almighty Father.

Weddings almost never include a collection, but they could. Some couples already jointly support a particular charity. They could invite participants to make a contribution to it on the occasion of their wedding. Or if they themselves wish to make a charitable donation to some cause in order to express their sacrifice of thanksgiving to God, it could be incorporated with the bread and wine presented at this time. A few couples request no wedding presents of their guests, especially if the arc of their lives and losses now brings them to a second or third wedding. By extension, they could request donations instead. Whatever the circumstances, if the arrival of this ceremony has inspired donations to charities, they can be included in the procession of the gifts.

15

Commemoration
in the Eucharistic Prayer

New to the second edition of the OCM is the inclusion of the
names of the couple in three of the eucharistic prayers. These
also appear in the Missal's ritual Mass for celebrating marriage.
Formerly the couple heard their names during the Liturgy of the Eucharist only if the priest offered Eucharistic Prayer I (the Roman Canon).

Tradition has long added to the Roman Canon a collection of special
petitions, one of which the priest inserts on certain occasions. The Missal
today calls for him to pronounce names during the eucharistic prayer on
occasions ranging from baptism to ordination. The community hears the
names of the pope and the local bishop in every eucharistic prayer, but
the names of others come more rarely. When the priest speaks names
aloud at this point of the Mass, he does not so much bestow an honor as
he identifies those who on this occasion rely on the community's prayers.
Even after the Second Vatican Council, the names of the couple could be
added only to Eucharistic Prayer I, but now they appear in Eucharistic
Prayers II and III as well.

Eucharistic Prayer IV has no such commemoration because its pref-
ace is never to be replaced, and the Missal's ritual Mass for celebrating
marriage comes with its own prefaces. Once the priest begins one of
them, he is not to switch to Eucharistic Prayer IV after the *Sanctus*. Instead, he turns to one of the first three. Therefore, Eucharistic Prayer IV
is not used in the Order of Celebrating Matrimony within Mass.

The commemoration of the couple in Eucharistic Prayer I specifically
asks God to accept the offering that this newly married couple is making
(202). This is especially appropriate if they have brought the gifts of

bread and wine to the altar during the Mass, and if they offer these gifts in the spirit of offering the service of their own lives. The community prays that God will grant gladness to these, his newly married servants.

The insert for Eucharistic Prayer II asks God to help the couple live in mutual love and peace (203). The commemoration in Eucharistic Prayer III prays for their faithfulness to marriage (204).

The commemoration of the couple may seem like a small feature, and it is easy for a priest to forget about it during the wedding Mass, but it is one way that the liturgy of the church places the couple in the very heart of its prayer.

16

The Nuptial Blessing

A highlight of any Catholic wedding is the nuptial blessing. Prior to the Second Vatican Council, the priest could offer it only during a Mass, and its words concerned the bride. Now a priest or deacon may offer the nuptial blessing even in a wedding without Mass, and the words pertain to both the bride and the groom.

For the first time ever in the Roman Rite these prayers now include an invocation for the Holy Spirit to come over the couple. These did not appear in the nuptial blessings immediately after the Second Vatican Council, but they have been inserted for the revised edition of the OCM. The first nuptial blessing now asks for the Holy Spirit, the gift of love, to help the couple remain faithful to the marriage covenant (74). The second nuptial blessing asks God to pour into the hearts of the couple the power of the Holy Spirit (207). The third asks that the power of the Holy Spirit set their hearts aflame, so that they may enrich the church (209). These blessings became available in the third edition of the Roman Missal's ritual Mass for celebrating marriage, and now they are even more accessible in the OCM. Each nuptial blessing is long, so the minister will need his oratorical skills to make them prayerful and to draw attention to the reference that each blessing makes to the Holy Spirit.

The nuptial blessing comes after the Lord's Prayer, and this timing often puzzles people. It seems as though this blessing should take place either after the exchange of rings, so that all the elements of marriage come together, or near the end of the Mass, where one normally expects to hear a blessing. In some parts of the world, the Vatican has authorized moving the nuptial blessing to another part of the Mass, but its traditional place is after the Lord's Prayer. Part of the reason is that prior to the council a Catholic wedding took place in church prior to the beginning of Mass. The wedding was preliminary to the Eucharist. However, the nuptial blessing assumed its place during the Mass as something more integral to the Eucharist.

Another reason for its location in the service is that the nuptial blessing has always enjoyed a place close to the eucharistic prayer. However, the Lord's Prayer owns the first position after the eucharistic prayer at every Mass. The faithful are standing in the real presence of Christ in the Eucharist, and the most perfect prayer that first comes to their lips is the one that Jesus himself taught. It is as though people want the risen Christ, truly present among them in sacramental signs, to hear that they are truly his disciples, and they have learned how he taught them to pray.

Consequently, as soon as spiritually possible after the consecration of the Eucharist, the priest offers a blessing over the couple. The nuptial blessing has more to do with the eucharistic prayer than with the Lord's Prayer. The couple's covenant participates in God's covenant with the church through Christ. Their blessing looks back to the eucharistic prayer and forward to communion. It links them to the great prayer of praise and consecration, and it prepares them for the peace and love they will share in the communion rite of the Mass.

New to the rubrics is a clarification that the couple either approach the altar or kneel at their place for this blessing (73). In practice, a priest may circle from his place behind the altar and reposition himself directly in front of the couple on the other side of the altar. However, there is no indication that he should move. Prior to the council, celebrating Mass at an altar attached to the wall, the priest had to turn and face the couple for this blessing. The rubric in the OCM that he stands and faces the bride and groom (72) is probably a holdover. Facing the people across the altar at Mass, he need not shift his position at this time. He may recite these words from the altar, which helps link the themes of covenant, blessing, and communion.

A musical setting of each blessing is included in the OCM (205–9). These follow a simple chant. The priest or deacon who sings these may add solemnity to the ceremony.

There are three options for the nuptial blessing, and the Introduction to the OCM identifies this as one of the parts of the wedding for which the couple may express a preference (29). During their marriage preparation, they would profitably study the words of the three options, meditate on them, and offer reasons why one may be more fitting than the others. This will prepare them to open their ears when the words are offered on their wedding day.

17

The Kiss

Photographers sometimes ask when to expect the couple to kiss during a Catholic wedding, so that they may capture the moment. The rubrics do not include a kiss in conjunction with the couple's exchange of consent, but at a wedding Mass the rubrics before Communion do invite the couple to offer "a sign that expresses peace and charity" (75).

Some couples may naturally want to kiss after the exchange of rings. They are married. They may wish to celebrate their joy. Nonetheless, cultural preferences may come to bear. In some societies it would be inappropriate for a man and a woman—even a married man and woman—to kiss in public. Perhaps the rubrics make no mention of a kiss after the couple's consent in order to ensure a solemn tone over the proceedings. If it seems appropriate, though, the couple could kiss after exchanging rings (67A), in keeping with the tolerance the rubrics hold for local customs (29).

The sign of peace during the communion rite, however, provides a more liturgical opportunity for an appropriate sign of unity and peace. In the moments before Communion, when the couple may be more accustomed to offering a sign of peace at Mass, they may more fittingly express their love just before receiving the primary sacrament of unity, the Body and Blood of Christ.

New to the second edition of the OCM is that sharing the sign of peace at a wedding Mass appears to be obligatory (75). The sign of peace is optional at a typical Mass. Most parish congregations have become quite comfortable sharing a sign of peace. Married couples may kiss; other worshipers usually shake hands. Many churchgoers feel that something is missing if the sign is not included. It is hard to imagine when a sign of peace is not appropriate before Communion. Nonetheless, the rubric in the Order of Mass says that the sign is offered at a typical Mass "if appropriate," allowing the possibility for the priest and deacon to omit it (128). Not, however, at a wedding. Now the rubric says that all present offer the sign. It is something they do. There is no question. If ever a sign expressing peace and charity were appropriate, it is at a wedding.

18

Communion Reserved for Catholics

T here has been no change in the legislation that only Catholics may receive Holy Communion at Mass (canon 844). Sometimes people wonder if exceptions can be made at a wedding. Specifically, may a non-Catholic who marries a Catholic receive Communion at the wedding Mass? May non-Catholic family members and friends receive? By itself, the wedding does not constitute an exception to the rule.

The Vatican's Directory for the Application of Principles and Norms on Ecumenism says that there are circumstances when non-Catholics may share Communion with Catholics, but there must be a grave and pressing need in the eyes of the local bishop (130–31). Also, the baptized person must be unable to have recourse to the sacrament in his or her own church, must ask for Communion on his or her own initiative, and believe what Catholics believe about the Eucharist.

This Directory admits that weddings between a Catholic and a baptized non-Catholic form a special case because the couple are sharing two other sacraments: baptism and marriage. Still, it says that the general norms must be observed (159–60).

Some priests make an announcement prior to the distribution of Communion to inform participants about the Catholic Communion rules. However, the United States Catholic Conference issued Guidelines for the Reception of Communion in 1996, and these are printed in the front of virtually every participation aid. The guidelines are probably already available at everyone's place in the parish church. If the couple are printing their own participation aid, they could reprint these for the sake of visitors. The guidelines can also be found online: http://www .usccb.org/prayer-and-worship/the-mass/order-of-mass/liturgy-of-the -eucharist/guidelines-for-the-reception-of-communion.cfm. They are somewhat complex, presenting separate paragraphs for Catholics, fellow Christians, those not receiving Communion, and non-Christians. A priest will probably keep the ceremony flowing if he avoids too much commentary and lets the printed guidelines lead the way.

The Introduction to the OCM for the first time references these canonical norms (36). Exceptions exist, but they are rare. For example, the baptized Christian may not have regular access to the Eucharist at all in his or her own tradition due to the distance to the nearest church and minister. But if that were the case, he or she could request permission to share Communion regularly at the Catholic Mass, not just on the wedding day.

There is another solution, of course, that the church recommends when a Catholic marries a baptized non-Catholic: weddings without Mass.

19

Weddings without Mass

Whenever a Catholic marries a baptized non-Catholic, the Order of Celebrating Matrimony without Mass should be used (36). However, the local bishop may permit marriage within Mass in these cases. He may even delegate that decision to his priests. But the celebration of matrimony without Mass for these ecumenical occasions is usually pastorally sound.

This legislation is not new, though it has not always been observed. Many Catholics assume that a Catholic wedding has to take place during Mass, but that is not true, nor is it always advisable.

Most importantly, the wedding is a celebration of the unity and equality of the two partners. If the ceremony takes place during Mass, and only the bride or the groom receives Communion, it signals an imbalance at the very summit of the Liturgy of the Eucharist between the couple who have just been joined as one. In addition, many of those attending the wedding will likely not know when to stand, kneel, or sit, nor how to make the responses. And only some will be eligible to receive Communion. This can make them feel more like observers than participants and witnesses in the celebration.

A wedding without Mass usually makes a better choice when a baptized non-Catholic marries a Catholic. It is the preference of the OCM. A wedding without Mass puts a diverse congregation on a more equal footing. All those present, especially those who follow Christ, will be nourished by the readings and prayers of the event. They can more uniformly fulfill their function as a community that witnesses and prays.

A priest or a deacon may preside for the Order of Celebrating Matrimony without Mass (79). A priest vests in alb and stole. He may wear a cope. He does not wear a chasuble; that vestment is reserved for Mass (and for the Celebration of the Passion of the Lord on Good Friday). If a deacon presides, he may wear alb and stole. He may also wear a dalmatic (80, 83). A cope or dalmatic would lend more solemnity to the ceremony.

The revised liturgical order is largely the same as its predecessor. It includes the introductory rites, the Liturgy of the Word, the marriage ceremony, and blessings. It omits the main elements of the Liturgy of the Eucharist: the preparation of the gifts, the eucharistic prayer, and elements of the communion rite. It may include a distribution of Communion; however, this may not be advisable for the same reasons that Mass is not.

Like the celebration of matrimony within Mass, this order presents two forms of the introductory rites (80–85). The entrance chant is only mentioned in the first form (80). In this form, the minister goes to the door of the church and greets the wedding party. The procession to the altar ideally is accompanied with music that people sing, thus accounting for the entrance chant. The second form makes no mention of the chant (84). It is hard to know if this is an oversight, if the second form presumes that there is no formal procession at all, or if the chant should also have been omitted from the first form because this is not Mass.

For a wedding within Mass, if the entrance antiphon or a hymn is not sung, someone should read the words aloud, as explained above. But since this ceremony happens without Mass, the rule does not apply. Still, the first form of the introductory rites explicitly calls for the chant, presumably even if it is recited, whereas the second form does not.

When all have reached their places, they make the sign of the cross, which is new to the second edition of the OCM. The minister gives the greeting, all respond (86), and then the minister gives an introduction. Two options are given (87–88), very similar to the two options that introduce a wedding within Mass. These are also new to the second edition of the OCM. The minister may use these or similar words.

The Liturgy of the Word takes place as it does for the Order of Celebrating Matrimony within Mass (90). One of the readings that speaks about marriage must be included. As mentioned above, these are marked with an asterisk.

The Table of Liturgical Days does not apply many restrictions to this circumstance. When a wedding takes place during Mass, the choice of readings and orations depends on the liturgical calendar, which governs the celebration of the Eucharist. Outside Mass, though, the rules of the calendar do not hold the same force. Hence, if a wedding without Mass takes place on a Saturday night during Easter Time, for example, the readings may all come from the wedding Lectionary. No reference to the liturgical day needs to be made.

After the homily the celebration of matrimony takes place as it does for the wedding within Mass (92–102). The same options exist for the exchange of consent, the giving of the rings, and the devotional custom of the *arras*.

As in the wedding within Mass, the congregation may sing an acclamation after the exchange of consent (99) and a hymn after the rings and the *arras* (102). These opportunities for song are new to the second edition of the OCM.

From this point, two different sequences happen depending on the decision concerning the distribution of Communion. Communion is permitted, but it may unintentionally underscore divisions more than unity. However, the wedding may be taking place in a part of the world where priests are scarce and the Mass is not celebrated every week. In such circumstances, when local Catholics do not have ready access to the Eucharist, the argument for distributing Communion outside of Mass becomes stronger.

The two possible sequences for the final parts of the wedding without Mass have only a minor adjustment. Here is the first possibility, which does not include Communion:

* The universal prayer (also called the prayer of the faithful) starts in the usual way with an introduction and the listing of intercessions. The nuptial blessing will be heard soon afterward, so the rubric makes an appeal that these petitions not repeat phrases from the blessing to come (103Ab). Normally at Mass, the priest concludes the universal prayer with an oration of his own, bringing the list of petitions to a conclusion. At a wedding without Mass and without Communion, he omits that final prayer.

* The Lord's Prayer comes after the petitions (103Ac). This parallels the format for the petitions at Morning and Evening Prayer in the Liturgy of the Hours, where the Lord's Prayer immediately follows the final intercession. It is not clear if the minister is supposed to introduce the Lord's Prayer by saying to the people words similar to those heard at Mass: "At the Savior's command / and formed by divine teaching, / we dare to say." An introduction between the petitions and the Lord's Prayer is included in the Liturgy of the Hours, so logically it

would be done here as well. The question arises because at Mass the universal prayer concludes with an oration by the priest without any intervention: The people have been praying, so he does not say, "Let us pray" before his final words. However, in this service, the petitions conclude when all the people are invited to pray the Lord's Prayer together. An introduction would cue them.

* The nuptial blessing follows the Lord's Prayer (104–5). This differs from the first edition of the OCM, which put the nuptial blessing before the Lord's Prayer in a wedding outside of Mass, even without Communion. This separated the nuptial blessing from the blessing of all the people. Now, when there is no Communion, the nuptial blessing follows the Lord's Prayer as it does for a wedding during Mass. The minister may use any of the three versions of the blessing. The placing of the *lazo* or the veil may precede the nuptial blessing, as in the wedding within Mass. The couple and the priest adopt the same postures and gestures as they would for the nuptial blessing at a wedding within Mass. Presumably the *lazo* or veil is removed at the conclusion of the blessing. The rubric mentions that this blessing is never omitted because before the Second Vatican Council it was not to be given on certain days and never outside of Mass. The blessing is so important that now it is given at every wedding.
* Following the nuptial blessing the minister blesses the full assembly (106). All may sing a final hymn (107). There is no sign of peace and no dismissal dialogue, as will be explained below.

When Communion is to be distributed, the second possible sequence of steps is observed. In this case, these steps maintain the unity of the communion rite by shifting the nuptial blessing to conclude the petitions. This keeps the blessing closer to the marriage ceremony. It also puts the distribution of Communion closer to the Lord's Prayer, which honors a distinct liturgical unit. The sequence for the second possibility is as follows:

* The universal prayer starts in the usual way with an introduction and the listing of the intercessions (103Aa). Again, the intercessions should not anticipate the wording of the nuptial blessing (103Ab), which in this case will follow immediately.
* The nuptial blessing concludes the universal prayer (104–5). It replaces the oration normally offered at the end of the universal prayer at Mass. The *lazo* or the veil may be blessed and positioned before the nuptial blessing begins (103B). The couple and the priest observe

the same postures and gestures mentioned for the nuptial blessing at Mass. The minister may use any of the three versions of the blessing. Presumably the *lazo* or veil, if used, is removed after the nuptial blessing.

* The minister goes to the place where the Eucharist is reserved, takes the ciborium of consecrated bread, and places it on the altar (108). Then he genuflects. He does not genuflect at the tabernacle. He genuflects once, at the altar, in the presence of the Blessed Sacrament there and in view of the people. No mention is made of the corporal, which is used during Mass to define the space where the gifts of bread and wine are placed for the offering of the sacrifice. The omission of the corporal indicates that no sacrifice is taking place at this time. (Similarly, the corporal is not mentioned in the ceremonies for distributing Communion outside of Mass nor for worship of the Eucharist outside of Mass. The vessel in those cases is similarly placed directly on the altar. The only exception to this is on Good Friday, when a corporal is placed on the altar for the distribution of Communion outside of Mass.)

* The minister introduces the Lord's Prayer (109), which clearly serves a different function than it does in the wedding without Mass and without Communion. Without Communion, the Lord's Prayer concludes the universal prayer and opens the way for the nuptial blessing. When Communion is to be distributed, the Lord's Prayer is not recited until the ciborium rests on the altar. Then, in the presence of the Body of Christ, disciples of Jesus Christ call upon their Father in the words Jesus taught them to use when they pray.

* The sign of peace is optional (110). The option only exists if Communion is to be distributed. The sign of peace is one of the signs of the communion of the people of God. It is exchanged at Mass as a declaration of their unity before they participate in the sacrament of Holy Communion. When Communion is not to be distributed, a sign of peace would not retain its purpose.

* The Lamb of God is omitted because this is not Mass. The Lamb of God accompanies the breaking of the bread, but bread was already broken at the Eucharist when this communion was consecrated.

* The minister genuflects (111). This is his second genuflection, and again it takes place before the Blessed Sacrament on the altar. This imitates the genuflection that the priest makes before he receives Communion at Mass. He then gives the same introduction that the priest normally gives at Mass, beginning with the words "Behold,

the Lamb of God." All those who are going to receive Communion respond with the prayer that begins, "Lord, I am not worthy," as at Mass.

* The minister distributes Communion to those who will receive (112). The rubrics do not indicate that the minister himself receives, nor do they include the private prayer that the priest makes before he receives Communion. By implication, then, the presider does not receive, especially if he is participating at Mass in another part of the day. Communion is distributed under only one form—the Body of Christ. Consecrated wine is not reserved in the tabernacle nor distributed at a service such as this.

* A song may be sung during the distribution of Communion (113). It is not required, again, because this is not Mass. The Missal includes a communion antiphon for every Mass, but this is different. This ceremony has no required antiphon. A congregational song about love, unity, or peace would be appropriate, though not obligatory. The first edition of the OCM imagined the possibility that only the bride and groom might be receiving Communion, but this vision has been removed from the second edition. If Communion is to be distributed, any qualified communicant may receive.

* After Communion there may be silence or a song of praise (114). Therefore, two songs may be sung in succession. If plans for the wedding include a soloist, it would be more appropriate for this person to sing the psalm or canticle of praise after Communion, allowing those who are sharing Communion to sing together a suitable hymn.

* The minister says a prayer after Communion and gives a final blessing (115–16).

Neither form of the wedding outside of Mass has a dismissal dialogue between the minister and the people like the one that always concludes a Mass. Probably this is because the Latin dismissal formula *Ite, missa est* is what gave birth to the English word "Mass." The Order of Mass in the Missal translates that command as "Go forth, the Mass is ended" (144). If such a formula had concluded this ceremony, it would have been confusing. In the Ceremonial of Bishops, when the bishop presides for a wedding without Mass, the deacon concludes with the dismissal, "Go in peace" (620). Perhaps this was an oversight, and it could have been inserted here to conclude the Order of Celebrating Matrimony without Mass, even if a deacon or priest presides.

Weddings between a Catholic and an Unbaptized Person

The OCM contains a special chapter for the marriage between a Catholic and a person who has never been baptized, whether that person is a catechumen or a nonbeliever (118–43). This option existed in the first edition, but it has a few additional features in the second.

When an unbaptized person has celebrated the Rite of Acceptance into the Order of Catechumens, his or her name should be recorded in the parish register of catechumens. If, sadly, a catechumen should die, he or she is entitled to Christian burial at the Catholic Church, even without ever having been baptized. More happily, if a catechumen becomes engaged, he or she may have a Catholic wedding, even if the other partner is not a Catholic. Whenever a Catholic and/or a catechumen marries, Chapter III of the OCM presents the proper order of service to be observed.

More commonly, though, Chapter III applies to the wedding of a Catholic with a person who is not a catechumen. Sometimes that person believes in Christ but has never been baptized. Other times the unbaptized person does not believe in Christ at all. Such a person may be content in his or her non-Christian belief, whether it is Judaism, Islam, Hinduism, atheism, or a host of other possibilities. Ever since the Second Vatican Council's Declaration on the Relation of the Church to Non-Christian Religions (*Nostra Aetate*), Catholics have worked hard to show respect to the beliefs of non-Christians.

One fruit of this dialogue is the Order of Celebrating Matrimony between a Catholic and a Catechumen or a Non-Christian. The title's inclusion of catechumens is new to the second edition of the OCM.

The ceremony may begin with the Rite of Reception (119). The ministers go to the door of the church to greet the wedding party. They enter and go to their seats. There is no sign of the cross and no greeting, because the rubrics assume that a sufficient number of non-Christians is present, people who could not participate in the trinitarian sign of the cross, nor honestly exchange the greeting, "The Lord be with you."

Instead, the ceremony begins with the celebrant's welcome (120). The welcome explains something about those who believe in God: "For believers, God is the source of love and fidelity, / because God is love." This declaration would be acceptable by Christian and non-Christian believers alike, and could help establish a common denominator among many participants at the wedding. The welcome has evangelical potential, but at the simplest level it helps everyone understand what is about to take place.

Nonetheless, even this introduction may be omitted if circumstances suggest (121). This is the only version of Catholic weddings that allows the ceremony to begin without any kind of greeting between the minister and the wedding party, any procession, congregational greeting, introduction, or oration. All the opening elements can be removed for an appropriate reason. If, for example, the number of nonbelievers overpowers the number of Christians, or the environment is hostile to believers, the opening ceremonies can be eliminated.

The Liturgy of the Word takes place as usual (122). However, the number of readings may be reduced to only one, and at least one reading must speak of marriage. That is, it must be drawn from the readings that carry an asterisk in the list. The reduction of the number of readings apparently aims to respect the diversity of beliefs present in the room, and to minimize the potential for alienation, while multiplying the opportunities for unity. Still, no provision is made for readings from any other source outside the Bible. With all due respect to people who do not share the Christian faith, the liturgy does not compromise this point: at least one passage from the Bible will be proclaimed. The Good News is also for them.

After the homily (123), the celebration of matrimony takes place. The presider gives an opening address, modeled on the one used for weddings within Mass (59). However, this one omits the reference to baptism and the declaration that marriage is a sacrament (124).

The questions before the consent and the words of consent do not change. For this part of the ceremony, no compromise is made on behalf of the nonbeliever. The Catholic is a believer, so the faith-filled language of the consent remains in place for that person's benefit (125–28). The minister receives the consent and invites the community to praise God with an acclamation (129–30).

For the exchange of rings, the minister blesses the rings as usual. However, the sprinkling of the rings with blessed water may be omitted (131), presumably if its connection to baptismal water might seem inappropriate to an unbaptized person. The couple exchange rings, but the non-Christian may omit speaking aloud the final words of this formula, which mention the Holy Trinity (132). In fact, the entire blessing and exchange of rings may be omitted (131). These symbols, so central to the traditional Catholic wedding, are not as important as the words of consent that the couple have already expressed.

The *arras* may be included after the rings (133). This may be especially important if the Catholic comes from a family tradition that participates in the culture of the *arras*, or if the unbaptized person is a catechumen from a similar tradition.

A hymn may be sung by all (134). Those planning the music should pay attention to the words and search for a hymn that invites the diverse people in the room to sing with authenticity. For example, some hymns are based on psalms that Christians may sincerely sing together with other believers who are accustomed to praying the Psalter.

The universal prayer follows (135), but at Mass this is considered to be an exercise of the baptized priestly people. In this ceremony outside Mass, all are invited to participate. Thus all the believers in the room may join in one voice to tell God their common concerns. If one of the samples from the first appendix is chosen (216 or 217), prudent editing will be necessary to remove the assumptions that Christians alone are offering these prayers. A better solution is to compose petitions in which other believers could join.

For the Lord's Prayer at this celebration, the OCM provides a carefully worded introduction (136). It invites the Christians present to call upon God as their Father. Then the Christians recite the prayer. This pays homage to the difference between those who are baptized and those who are not. The circumstance is enshrined in a ceremony within the Rite of Christian Initiation of Adults, in which those preparing for baptism receive the Presentation of the Lord's Prayer, normally in the final weeks or hours before their initiation. After they have been baptized, having been adopted as children of God, they more legitimately call God their Father. They pray the Lord's Prayer together with all the faithful at the Easter Vigil in the moments after their baptism and before their First Communion. Thus, the Lord's Prayer is the prayer of Christians. It binds them as brothers and sisters who share a common inheritance under the God whom Jesus invited them to call "Father." At a wedding where non-Christians are present, they may remain silent while the Christians recite their own prayer of baptismal adoption, ecclesial unity, and faithful discipleship.

The *lazo* or veil may be placed on the couple before the nuptial blessing (137). Again, these customs probably make more sense if the unbaptized person is a catechumen from a culture that honored these traditions, or if the Catholic comes from such a family.

As a rule, the nuptial blessing follows (138–39). This version does not mention the couple's sharing of communion. Even so, the entire nuptial blessing can be replaced with a shorter prayer (140). With these words the minister asks God to uphold the marital institution established for the gift of children, and to keep safe this couple's union. For whatever reason, if this shorter prayer seems more appropriate, it may be used. If the couple have worn the *lazo* or the veil, presumably they are removed after the nuptial blessing.

The presider blesses all present with the sign of the cross (141). This is done for the benefit of the Christians. A song may conclude the celebration (142).

As in the wedding outside Mass, there is no dismissal of the people. The traditional formulas have more to do with sending forth into the world the people who have just shared communion together.

The number of marriages between Catholics and unbaptized persons may well be increasing, so the publication of this particular order of service is timely. It may at times appear inconsistent while it attempts to please all participants, but it strives to balance respect for nonbelievers with sincere expression of Christian faith. It aims to achieve the goals of interfaith dialogue, articulating one's own belief, while allowing the belief—and nonbelief—of others.

21

The Deacon as Presider

Adeacon may preside for a Catholic wedding. The normal ceremony he leads is Chapter II, The Order of Celebrating Matrimony without Mass, unless the marriage includes a person who has never been baptized. In that case, he leads Chapter III, The Order of Celebrating Matrimony between a Catholic and a Catechumen or a Non-Christian.

The deacon vests in an alb and stole, and he may wear the dalmatic over them (80). No rubrics forbid him to use the presider's chair.

At times people may ask a deacon to witness a marriage (or perform a baptism) that takes place within Mass celebrated by a priest. The request arises because sometimes the deacon is related to the bride or groom or has been friends with them. Or in his ministry he has completed the preparation for the couple, and people wish him to preside over the sacrament for them.

The rubrics for a wedding within Mass call upon the priest to preside. They do not imagine a situation in which the deacon would serve as the church's official witness during Mass. A deacon may preside for a baptism or a wedding outside of Mass (canons 816 §1 and 1108 §1), but may he do so within a Mass?

In another context, the *Book of Blessings* states, "It belongs to the ministry of a *deacon* to preside at those blessings that are so indicated in place in this book . . . But whenever a priest is present, it is more fitting that the office of presiding be assigned to him and that the deacon assist by carrying out those functions proper to the diaconate" (18).

From this, it appears that normally the priest who presides at a liturgy presides over all its parts, including blessings, baptisms, and matrimony. However, the *Book of Blessings* says that having a priest preside for an entire service is "more fitting" than having a deacon lead a part of it for him. It may be less "fitting" for a deacon to bless while a priest presides, but it is not forbidden.

The same principle may apply to weddings. There may be places, for example, where priests are scarce, and the Eucharist is not often cele-brated. A deacon who is the spiritual leader of a local community may wish to preside for a wedding even when the priest is making one of his visits. Or perhaps the couple and the deacon speak a language that the priest does not. Or, as mentioned above, the deacon may be a relative or friend of the couple.

Opinions differ on this question, but deacons in fact commonly do preside for baptisms and weddings during Mass. The church's law does not expressly forbid it. The rubrics make no explicit accommodation for it. It is best seen as the exception, rather than the rule.

22

The Marriage Record

At the conclusion of the wedding, whether or not it takes place during Mass, the witnesses and the minister sign the marriage record (78, 117, 143). This action should not be carried out on top of the altar.

This rubric, new to the second edition of the OCM, appears to refer to the parish marriage record, not the civil marriage license. In some countries it is customary for the witnesses and the minister to sign the parish marriage record. In the United States, it is more common for a secretary to enter the names in the parish office during business hours a few days after the ceremony.

The minister and the witnesses do sign the civil marriage license in the United States. However, in the Catholic Church, some church weddings are ecclesial convalidations of civil ceremonies that took place sometime prior. In that case, no new civil document is drawn up or signed, but the parish marriage record is still made.

The main point of this rubric is to keep the action off the top of the altar. The top, sometimes called the *mensa* or the table, is particularly holy to the Catholic liturgy. It receives the sacred cloths and vessels, the Missal, and possibly a cross and the candles for Mass—though not the unity candle at a wedding, if this has been included in the ceremony. In fact, no other items should rest on the altar, not even flowers (GIRM 305). Actions not associated with the liturgy should take place elsewhere, and signing the marriage record is an example.

If the minister and witnesses sign the civil license after the ceremony, they may do it in the sacristy, the office, or even some visible space in the church—but not on top of the altar.

23

Marriage Preparation and the Wedding Rehearsal

Working backwards from the ceremony as outlined in the second edition of the OCM, those responsible for marriage preparation will see some matters to discuss with the engaged couple:

The first eleven paragraphs of the Introduction of the OCM give an overview of the Catholic theology of matrimony. As catechumens study the Creed before they are baptized, so engaged couples may study these paragraphs to learn what the Catholic Church teaches about the way of life to which they are called. The paragraphs are dense, but with help, the couple should be able to understand them. They will surely find an articulation of the values that they themselves share as they prepare the wedding day.

A presentation on the wedding procession could help couples better understand one of the principal signs of the Catholic service. The bride and groom may already have the order of procession fixed in their minds long before they begin marriage preparation at the parish, but they can still receive education about the difference and opportunities in the Catholic wedding procession.

Couples generally need guidance on music for a Catholic wedding. If the parish ministers and musicians have agreed on some guidelines and suggestions, they can share these in the light of the musical opportunities presented in the OCM.

The OCM invites the couple to have a voice in the selection of the readings and prayers. They will need access to these options, along with some help interpreting the relevance of each selection. The task takes work, but it will reward them with deeper reflection on the words of the wedding.

When a Catholic marries another Christian, the church recommends celebrating a wedding without Mass. Before wedding plans are set, couples may need to hear why this is important, along with the reassurance that the ceremony without Mass is still a binding, sacramental wedding in the church.

Someone may help the couple understand the parish's financial expectations. The couple will want to know what donations, if any, are recommended or expected by the parish, the clergy, the musicians, sacristans, servers, or any other ministers. The OCM gives no guidance, and policies change from one parish to another.

The Order of Blessing an Engaged Couple may be included in preparation. This could be offered in a family home or in a room at church. The order of service is in the second appendix of the OCM.

Some other matters pertain to the wedding rehearsal. Not every couple has one, but if they do, here are some thoughts to bear in mind:

Close family members will want to know where they are to sit. The OCM gives no guidance, so the couple will have to think this through. Often someone from the parish can give advice. The couple will want to give special attention to close family members affected by death or divorce.

If the wedding will not include Mass, Catholics attending the rehearsal may appreciate knowing why this is so.

The one leading the rehearsal may give everyone catechesis on the wedding procession, especially if the priest will greet both the bride and groom at the door of the church, and if the couple enter together.

The rehearsal will naturally focus on the procession and the staging of the wedding party for the exchange of consent. Simple, clear directions will help them feel confident.

However, the liturgy expects more of the wedding party. They are invited to participate by singing the songs and making the responses, as well as by listening to the readings and the prayers. Because they will be so visible during the ceremony, they have an important opportunity to lead all present by their example. Encouraging their participation will help them turn their minds and thoughts to God during the ceremony at the church.

A rehearsal can guide the couple to exchange their consent in a full, confident voice. This will help everyone else fulfill their role as witnesses. If desirable, microphones could be set in place. If the couple will read the words of their consent and the exchange of rings from the OCM, instead of repeating their lines after the minister, they may practice, holding their right hands, looking at their partner, reading from the book, and speaking into a microphone. They could read any words from the OCM at the rehearsal; they need not practice the actual words of consent. Those may be reserved for the wedding.

All liturgical ministers will hope to receive clear instructions. Often the couple want to invite family or friends to help as altar servers, readers, and communion ministers. If, for example, the altar servers are unacquainted with the church or the priest, they may take some time at the rehearsal or on another occasion to familiarize themselves with the sacristy and sanctuary. Readers will want to know where to find the reading in the Lectionary and how to activate the microphone. Ushers should know the location of the restrooms and first aid. Communion ministers will seek directions on where to stand to receive Communion themselves and to distribute it to others. Musicians will want access to pertinent parish guidelines.

The rehearsal can be a positive experience for all. A representative from the parish may welcome the wedding party at the beginning and invite them to return for worship on another day. If a priest is available, he may offer to hear confessions or just lend an ear to those who are troubled—or to those who rejoice. Some people may take this opportunity to reactivate their participation in Catholic life or to learn more about what the church has to offer. Many of those who prepare weddings for a parish feel burdened by the task, but each wedding provides an opportunity for evangelization and joy.

24

Participation Aid

I n preparing the ceremony, many couples, parish offices, and wedding planners want to print a participation aid for the people who will attend. An aid can even be made available through electronic media. The OCM offers no explicit guidance, but in the light of its revisions, the aid should include several points to help the congregation take an active role in the celebration.

Ministers. Many couples like to list the members of the wedding party, making the participation aid a keepsake, as well as a helpful tool to build a sense of unity among the people gathered together for this occasion. It would fittingly include the names of any of the liturgical ministers for the celebration.

Music. A participation aid may include the numbers of hymns and acclamations as they are found in a hymnal or booklet in the pew. Or, if copyright permissions have been obtained, the music may be reprinted in a leaflet specially prepared for the wedding. The music could include an opening hymn, the Gloria, the responsorial psalm, the gospel acclamation, the acclamation after the couple's consent, the hymn of praise after the rings, and the other acclamations and hymns that one usually experiences throughout the Liturgy of the Eucharist at a Sunday Mass. In a wedding without Mass, of course, some of this eucharistic music is omitted.

Postures. A participation aid may indicate when the people should stand, sit, and kneel. Special attention can be given to the entrance procession. In a Catholic ceremony, a congregation should stand from the beginning of the procession, not when the bride enters the aisle. The aid may tell the congregation that they are to stand for the actual celebration of matrimony after the gospel and homily. As the couple answer questions and exchange their consent, the people stand because they are witnesses of this action to all they meet.

Communion. The aid should either reproduce the Guidelines for the Reception of Communion provided by the United States Catholic Conference, or indicate where these can be found in another resource. This will provide hospitality to those who want to honor the practices of the Catholic Church and promote the participation that the OCM desires.

Contact information. Sometimes the couple include their future address and contact information in the participation aid. It would be a courtesy to include similar information for the parish church: its name, address, phone number, office email address, and website. If visitors to the church like what they find, they may wish to return. A wedding can build relationships.

Photography. Some parishes have photography policies. Since many people carry cameras or cellular devices in pockets and purses, participants as well as professional photographers will appreciate knowing the local rules. If the parish does not want photographers to enter the sanctuary where they may distract, or stand in the center aisle where they may block the view of others, or approach too close to the couple as they exchange their consent, the participation aid can put prudent guidance into everyone's hands. Professional photographers appreciate knowing the local rules because they'd like to be welcomed back. Photography guidelines help maintain order in the ceremony, but they also remind the community of the role that everyone plays. The ceremony relies on the liturgical participation and prayerful witness of everyone in the room—even of the photographers.

Cellular devices. The participation aid may remind people to switch off their cellular devices and anything that might produce noise during the ceremony. Their cooperation will provide a more prayerful atmosphere for everyone else, and will invite them to concentrate more fully on the wedding.

Once the aids are printed, they should be given not only to the people who occupy the pews but also to the wedding party, the bride, and the groom. They may all carry the aids in procession, singing the opening hymn. Or someone may set the leaflets at their places before the ceremony begins. In this way, the wedding party can set an example of prayerful participation in *The Order of Celebrating Matrimony.*

25

Anniversaries

On the anniversary of marriage a couple may wish to celebrate part of their day with the worshiping community at church. In this way they may give thanks to God for preserving their union and guiding them along the way. They also bear witness to the joys of marriage and provide hope for other couples.

In the past it has been common for couples to repeat their consent on such occasions, essentially replaying the words they spoke on their wedding day. The Catholic Church never officially endorsed this practice because the original consent is permanent by design and does not bear repeating. The *Book of Blessings* has always included Orders for the Blessing of a Married Couple (90–134), which instruct the couple to renew their commitment in silence (96, 109, and 123). However, this was often overlooked, creating a void into which stepped the practice of repeating the consent.

The third appendix of the OCM now offers a more expanded ceremony for the occasion of an anniversary. It fills a pastoral need. It does not include a repetition of the consent, but rather an optional expression of thanksgiving for the marriage. It is called the Order of Blessing a Married Couple within Mass on the Anniversary of Marriage. The suggested occasion is the twenty-fifth, fiftieth, or sixtieth anniversary (237).

The choice of readings and prayers follows rules a little different from those of a wedding Mass. The anniversary celebration is not a sacrament, so it does not hold the same weight against the Table of Liturgical Days. In general, if the celebration takes place on a weekday in Ordinary Time that does not rank as a feast or solemnity, the priest may use the prayers from the Roman Missal from the Mass called On the Anniversaries of Marriage, which is number 11 in the collection of Masses for Various

Needs and Occasions near the back of the book. The readings may come from the same section of the fourth volume of the Lectionary (943–47). The GIRM offers explicit details governing the Mass to be celebrated on this day (376). However, at any celebration, even a Sunday Mass when the Missal's prayers On the Anniversaries of Marriage cannot be used, the priest may fully celebrate the OCM's Order of Blessing a Married Couple within Mass on the Anniversary of Marriage.

The ceremony begins after the homily. The couple probably enter the sanctuary, though the rubrics do not indicate where they are. The priest invites them to renew in silence their commitment "to live their Marriage in holiness" (240). They do so quietly (241).

Or, they may recite aloud the new words from the ritual (242). These are based on the original words of consent. As on their wedding day they each said to the other, "I take you" as a spouse, now on their anniversary they each praise God for the spouse they "took." Again, recalling the consent, they thank God for being their companion "in the good times and the bad times," and for helping them to remain faithful. The priest concludes this thanksgiving with a prayer.

The next section is called "The Blessing of Rings," though the prayers are really for the couple. Two possibilities are proposed. In the first, the priest asks God to increase and sanctify the love of the couple who gave each other the rings as a sign of their faithfulness (243). The prayer is similar to one of the options for the blessing of rings in the wedding Mass (195). At the anniversary celebration, a rubric says that "the rings may be honored with an incensation" (243). It is not clear from the ritual if the couple are expected to remove their rings and set them on a stand, or if they keep them on and present their hands for the prayer and optional incensation. Local circumstances will probably determine this. Obviously, if incense is to be used, it will have to be lighted sometime earlier than this, and perhaps used throughout the Mass at the usual times.

The second possibility is for the couple to present new rings to each other (244). In this case the priest offers a prayer that these rings remind the couple of their love "and recall the grace of the Sacrament." Alternatively, the priest may bless these rings with one of the options from the wedding Mass (194). The ritual is silent after this, so it is not clear what happens next with the rings. If new rings were blessed, the couple will want to present them to each other. The ritual offers no words for them to say, but the placing of new blessed rings in silence is probably symbol enough.

There is no mention of the cultural symbols of the *arras*, the *lazo*, or the veil. These customs pertain to the wedding day.

The universal prayer (the prayer of the faithful) follows (245). A sample is provided, but a new set of intentions may be composed for the occasion. The priest concludes these intercessions as usual (246).

During the Liturgy of the Eucharist the couple may bring the gifts to the altar (247). After the Lord's Prayer, the priest offers the couple a blessing (248). The timing and tone resemble those of the nuptial blessing. A reference to children is optional, in order to accommodate the situation in which the couple have no children of their own.

For the end of the celebration, the priest may offer a solemn blessing (251). The one that appears in the ritual is based on one of the options for a wedding (214), though it omits the reference to the future blessing of children.

This ceremony is a pastorally satisfying expression of the joy families experience when a married couple reach a significant milestone. It pays respect to the wedding day without duplicating it, it thanks God for blessings received, it encourages other married couples, and it opens the vista to future glory.

Every engaged couple longs to see a major anniversary. Filled with love on their wedding day, they look forward to every future day, spent in union with the love of their lives. They have come to church because they believe in God, they want to thank God for their blessings, and they realize that the life they are about to undertake is something bigger than what humanity alone can express or support. In their personal love they have touched something eternal, something that finds its home in a church, and something that deserves anniversaries. They gain new entrance into the great mystery of God, who is love, who shares love with them, and who helps them transcend good times and bad. They can do all this because they partake of one love.

Index

Also by the Author

Inseparable Love: The Order of Celebrating Matrimony in the Catholic Church. Collegeville, MN: Pueblo, 2017.

Ministry & Liturgy *Bulletin Inserts.* Vol. 4. San Jose, CA: Resource Publications, 2012.

Preparing the Wedding Homily: A Guide for Preachers and Couples. San Jose, CA: Resource Publications, 2003.

The Catholic Wedding Answer Book: Ministry & Liturgy *Answers the 101 Most-Asked Questions.* San Jose, CA: Resource Publications, 2001.